THE PLIGHT OF MAN

&

THE POWER OF GOD

The Plight of Man

&

the Power of God

~

Dr Martyn Lloyd~Jones

CHRISTIAN
HERITAGE

Dr. Martyn Lloyd-Jones (1899-1981) was born in Wales. He was a dairyman's assistant, a political enthusiast, debater, and chief clinical assistant to Sir Thomas Harder, the King of England's Physician. But at the age of 27 he gave up a most promising medical career to become a preacher... When a spiritual history of the 20th century comes to be written it will be bound to include mention not only the far-reaching influence of Dr. Lloyd-Jones' ministry at Westminster Chapel in London, England from 1938-68, but of the remarkable fact that his published volumes of expository sermons have had an unprecedented circulation for such material, selling in millions of copies.

Unless otherwise indicated all Scripture quotations are taken from the Holy Bible, the King James Version.

ISBN 978-1-84550-439-7

© Martyn Lloyd - Jones

10 9 8 7 6 5 4 3 2 1

Published in 2009
Reprinted in 2010
by
Christian Focus Publications, Ltd.,
Geanies House, Fearn, Ross-shire,
IV20 1TW, Great Britain.

www.christianfocus.com

Cover design by Daniel Van Straaten

Printed by Norhaven, Denmark

CONTENTS

~
Foreword
~

"Saved from what?!" He slowly swaggered his answer, with all his weight landing slowly and surely on that last word, as if to physically push the person back. The "person" was an evangelical Christian sharing the Gospel. And the one responding with the "Saved from what?" was a minister in his 60's. I was a bit shocked when I first heard this man tell his story of his brush with the evangelist. After all, he was a minister. He should know what we need to be saved from. But he didn't. He really didn't. And he exulted in the fact that he had pushed back so directly against his would-be evangelist. I wish I had had a copy of this book then.

What is the Gospel? Can you summarize it? Is it any different than the Gospel your Christian grandparents would have believed? In these five messages (originally delivered in Edinburgh in March, 1941) Dr. David Martyn

Lloyd-Jones, celebrated pastor of Westminster Chapel, London, gives the answer. And I am struck by the clarity and power of his preaching.

These messages show the powerfully critical mind the Lord gave Dr. Lloyd-Jones (or simply "The Doctor" as he was affectionately and respectfully known). Here he lays out the history of philosophy, psychology, politics, along with the history of Bible times and of the church. He thinks comprehensively and yet succinctly and clearly. And that clarity of thought translates well to the printed page.

The brevity of this book only adds to its punch.

In these messages, Dr. Lloyd-Jones lays bare the pretensions of those who would reject or attempt to modify Biblical Christianity. With analytic clarity and gospel-power, the Doctor investigates the second half of Romans 1.

Written against the backdrop of war, Lloyd-Jones dismisses the lamentable ignorance of those who affirm the reality of human goodness, and who view war as an aberration from our natural state. Romans 1 contradicts this entirely, Lloyd-Jones says. The Doctor shows that our view of man is fundamental. In "The Religious History of Mankind" Lloyd-Jones entirely disagrees with the history of religions school, and any idea that man is getting better. He looks at Romans and at human history and says that the clear message is that we are in spiritual trouble.

In his second message, "Religion and Morality" he looks at how morality must follow from, and be preceded by religion. This is against the trend today to attempt to have morality without religion. Such a disordering is a mistake with profound implications not least of which is the withering of the very morality which is being exalted. Morality is not self-sustaining. When the Gospel goes, good deeds are not far behind.

The entire third message is taken up with the doctrine of sin, a doctrine which Lloyd-Jones identifies as among the most hated and ridiculed of all Christian doctrines. What is our greatest problem? Sin. The Doctor outlines competing theories of human nature, and shows some of their inadequacies. Sin, he says, following Paul's argument, is deliberate, debasing and disgusting. Romans 1 is as piercing today as it was in the 1940s.

The first three messages lead us down into the pit. They explore our dire situation. And they lead us to the fourth, on "The Wrath of God." Lloyd-Jones is explicit in his depiction of God's wrath against sin. Drawing from both Testaments, he makes it clear that sentimentalized views distort the Biblical picture of God. Only faithfully representing God's commitment to justice and holiness can properly inform our understanding of His love.

These were the four messages Lloyd-Jones gave. At the time, he said he felt like they needed a fifth, finally focusing more positively on "The Only Solution." And so, when it came time for publication, Dr. Lloyd-Jones supplied an extra, final chapter. As a summary of the Gospel, few chapters will serve you better.

On the whole, what we have in these five expositions is the Gospel explained with great clarity and hope. Even today I used these timeless chapters with a non-Christian friend who is seeking to understand Christianity. I commend these messages to you.

May reading these chapters encourage you in the Gospel, and in sharing it with others.

Mark Dever,
Capitol Hill Baptist Church, Washington, DC

~ *Chapter One* ~

The
Religious
History
of
Mankind

~ Chapter One ~
The Religious History of Mankind

Romans 1:21

> 'Because that, when they knew God, they glorified him
> not as God, neither were thankful; but became vain in
> their imagination, and their foolish heart was darkened.'

We are all familiar with the saying which reminds us that
there are times when we have 'to be cruel to be kind'. And
we know how that truth has to be applied in the realm of
training children or in dealing with someone who is ill. The
conditions may be such that the best interest of the child or
patient is served by causing temporary pain. It is a difficult
task for the parent or the doctor, a task from which he shrinks
and which he tries to avoid to the uttermost. But if he has the
real interest of the other at heart he just has to do it.

Now that, it seems to me, is the principle which the Church is called upon to put into practice at the present time, if she is to function truly as the Church of God in this hour of crisis and calamity. That she shrinks from doing so (and let us remember that there is no such thing as the Church apart from ourselves who compose and constitute the Church) is as evident as it is in the case of individuals. It is always more pleasant to soothe and to comfort than to cause pain and to arouse unpleasant reactions.

But surely the time has arrived when the situation of the world today must be dealt with and considered in a radical manner.

Nothing could be more fatal than for the impression to get abroad that the one business of the Church is to soothe and to give comfort to men and women who have been rendered unhappy by the present circumstances. I say the 'one business', for, of course, we all must thank God for the marvellous and wondrous consolation which the gospel alone can give. But if we give the impression that that is the only function of the Church, then we partly justify the criticism levelled at her that her main function is to supply a kind of 'dope' to the people. At first, under the immediate shock of war, it was essential that we should be steadied and comforted; but if the Church continues to do nothing but this, then surely we give the impression that our Christianity is something which is very weak and lifeless. The ministry of comfort and consolation is a part of the work of the Church, but if she devotes the whole of her energy to that task alone, as she did in general during the last war, she will probably emerge from this present trouble with her ranks still more depleted and counting for still less in the life of the people.

In the same way, if she contents herself with nothing beyond vague general statements designed to help and to encourage the national effort – if she but tries to add a spiritual gloss to the statements and speeches of the secular leaders of the country – while she may gain a certain amount of temporary applause and popularity and find herself being employed by the powers that be, in the end she will stand discredited in the eyes of the discerning.

Apart from anything else, for the Church to be content with either of these two attitudes, or with a combination of both, is for her to place herself in a purely negative position. She is merely palliating symptoms instead of dealing positively and actively with the disease. She is simply trying to tide over the difficulties, or, to change the metaphor, she is a mere accompanist instead of being the soloist. She is replying to a statement instead of issuing the challenge, and thereby appears as if she is somewhat frightened and bewildered. In the same way, and here I speak more especially to those of us who are Evangelicals, we must not continue with our religious life and methods precisely as if nothing were happening round and about us, and as if we were still living in the spacious days of peace. We have loved certain methods. And how delightful they were! What could be more enjoyable than to have and to enjoy our religion in the form in which we have for so long been familiar? How enjoyable just to sit and listen. What an intellectual and perhaps also emotional and artistic treat. But alas! How entirely unrelated to the world in which we live it has often been! How little has it had to offer to men and women who have never known our background and our kind of life, who are entirely ignorant of our very idiom and even our presuppositions. But in any case how detached and self-contained, how remote from a world that is seething in trouble with the foundations of everything that has been most highly prized rocking and shaking.

We must rouse ourselves and realize afresh that though our gospel is timeless and changeless, it nevertheless is always contemporary. We must meet the present situation and we must speak a word to the world that none else can speak.

There are many reasons why we should do so. The need of the world, its agony, its pain, its disease, call upon us to do so. But apart from that, it is our duty to do so. It is a part of the original commission given to the Church. She is a debtor in the sense in which St Paul so describes himself in the fourteenth verse of this chapter. There are indeed some who would say that if the Church fails in this present crisis, that if she does not realize that her very existence is at stake, the main result of the present troubled state of the world will be the end of the Church. That is a proposition from which I thoroughly dissent. The Church will continue because she is the Church of God and because He will sustain her until her work is completed. But if we fail we may well find the Church weakened in numbers and in power to a degree that has not been true of her for many a long century. And, above all, we shall have been traitors to the cause.

We must deal with the present position as it is. But the way in which we do so is of vital importance. And that is why I say that we must be prepared to 'be cruel to be kind'.

If we are anxious to help and to speak the redeeming word, we must first of all probe the wound and reveal the trouble. This cannot be done without giving rise to pain and perhaps also to offence. And that, in turn, will lead to our being unpopular and disliked in a sense that can never be true of us if we are merely soothing the world, or else more or less ignoring it entirely, whilst we enjoy our own religion. I would say again that her failure in general to deal vitally and realistically with the situation during the last war is one of the saddest chapters in the history of the Christian Church.

That must not be repeated, whatever it may cost. The last war was regarded as a kind of interlude in the drama of life, and men, failing to realize that it was an essential and inevitable part of the drama itself, just waited for it to end that they might resume at the point at which they suddenly left off in August, 1914. The real problem was not faced. But surely the history of the past twenty years and the present scene must force us to face the problem. Our attitude must not just be one of waiting for the war to end in order that we may resume our normal activities. We must be more active than we have ever been before and especially in our thinking.

The great central question is this. Why is the world in its present condition? But this must be considered very particularly in the light of the teaching concerning life that has been most popular during the past hundred years. That things are as they are is bad enough. But when we contrast them with the bright and optimistic pictures of life which have been held before us so constantly, the problem becomes heightened. The war of 1914-18, as has been said, was regarded as but a strange and inexplicable pause in the forward march of human progress. The progress was to be continued after the war. And here we are in our present circumstances! How can all this be explained? What is the cause of the trouble?

Surely it must be obvious by now that that whole view of life was entirely wrong and false? But is it? Is it obvious to all of us who claim to be Christians? Have not many of us rejoiced for years in what we fondly regarded as the inevitable progress of the world? Have we not felt within ourselves that, in spite of dwindling Church membership and attendance, and in spite of the obvious deterioration in the general tone of life, the world was nevertheless a better place? While the world has been gradually but certainly drifting to its present position, the voice of the majority, far from issuing warnings of alarm, has rather been rejoicing in the wonderful achievements of man and the dawning of a wondrous new era in human history.

There can be but one explanation of that: such a view of life must be tragically and fundamentally wrong.

It is in order to expose that fallacy, and to reveal the truth, that I call your attention to this second half of the first chapter of the Epistle to the Romans. I know of no passage in Scripture which describes so accurately the world of today and the cause of the trouble. Indeed, there is nothing in contemporary writing which so perfectly describes the present scene. It is a terrible passage. Melancthon described the eighteenth verse as 'an exordium terrible as lightning.' And it has not only the terrifying quality of lightning, but also its illuminating power. I am anxious to consider it with you, as it reveals some of the common underlying fallacies that have been responsible for the false view of life that has deluded mankind for so long.

The first matter that must engage our attention is the view of man himself, and especially in his relationship to God.

There is no need to indicate how this matter is quite fundamental. For our whole approach to man and his problems will depend upon our view of man. And nowhere, perhaps, is the complete antithesis between the biblical view and the popular view of the last years more evident than here. The second half of the last century will always be remembered as a period of immense intellectual activity and of scientific research. Even yet we are not perhaps fully aware of all the changes which were wrought as the result of that effort. But surely nothing was more remarkable as a direct result of all this than the entire change which took place in the view held of man. We are not concerned at the moment, and have not time to deal with the general question of the new view that came into vogue of man's origin and development. We are interested rather in the new view that came into being with respect to man's relationship to God. At the same time, we would indicate that the same general controlling principle held sway here as in the other matter – the principle of growth and development. That principle indeed can be found running through all the views of life and of man that gained currency during that period. In the realm of religion this whole tendency gave rise to a new science, or what was termed a science – namely, the study of comparative religion. This arose partly as the result of the colonizing movements of the previous century and partly also as a result of the facts that came to light in connection with the work of the various missionary societies. Wherever men went they discovered that the natives and the savages all had some form or other of religion. Gradually they began to note these religions and to take special interest in noting the type of religion found in relation to the type of people amongst whom it was found. Eventually, on the basis of all this, a theory was propounded, to the effect that a definite and certain evolution and development was to be found in the history of man in a religious sense. The steps and stages were clearly marked out as one passed from the most primitive to the most highly developed form. We cannot enter into the details, but by those who belonged to this school we were told that man in his most primitive form believed in a vague spirit that was resident in trees and stones and other objects – animism. Then came a kind of magic, then ancestor worship and totemism, ghost worship, fetishism, etc., until a stage was reached which could be described as polytheism – the state of affairs found in Greece and Rome in the time of our Lord – and eventually from that to the belief in one-God monotheism. All this was meant to show how there is innate in man a law which causes him to seek for God and to reach out for Him. In the most primitive and unintelligent type, we are told, it is present, and as man grows and develops and progresses the idea becomes more and more purified and noble, until we eventually arrive at the belief of the Jews in a holy and just God. Indeed, those who held this view argued that what they were thus able to elaborate as a theory on the basis of their observed data was also confirmed by what was to be found in the Old Testament itself. There, they said, could be seen clearly a gradual development in the idea of God held by the Children of Israel. The important point is that this theory presupposes that man by nature is a creature who is ever seeking and thirsting for a knowledge of God and for communion with Him, and that Christ is the Man who has penetrated furthest and reached highest in that endeavour. To some, of course, this theory just proved that God was really non-existent, and that the development which is to be observed is nothing but a gradual refining and improving, and an attempt to give intellectual respectability to what was originally a myth arising on the basis of the fear of life.

That, then, is the theory and view that has held sway. What have we to say to it?

I am directing your attention to this passage in Romans 1 in order that we may see how false this view is. We can arrange our matter under the following headings:

(i) It is a view which is false to biblical history. St Paul reminds the Romans, and therefore us, that the actual facts entirely disprove this theory. He is out to show that the whole world is guilty before God. He does so by showing that all are without excuse. The way in which he demonstrates this is to show that at the commencement God, having made man, revealed Himself to him. He not only revealed His eternal power and Godhead in nature and in creation, from which all men ought to reason to the fact of God, but He further has placed within man, in his very nature, a knowledge and an intimation and a sense of God which should lead man to God. Man, says St Paul, started with the knowledge of God, and if he lacks it now it is because he has deliberately suppressed and lost it. The story of man with respect to God, according to the Apostle, is not one of gradual progress and development and rising, but rather one of decline and fall – retrogression.

And, surely, any fair reading of the Old Testament shows this to be the case. Man starts in communion with God and in a state of happiness. It is as a result of his own action, his own sin, that that communion is broken and man's problems begin. For a while this knowledge and recognition of God continued and persisted, but as we read the story we can see it becoming more and more dim. And as the knowledge of God becomes less, so the life deteriorates. I would remind you that even Abraham was brought up in a state of idolatry. Even the special line of Shem had deteriorated and had wandered away from this true knowledge of God. But then God takes hold of Abraham and gives him the special revelation of Himself. This is transmitted to Isaac and to Jacob and then to the Children of Israel. But what happens to them? You have but to read their story to see that there is ever in them precisely the same tendency as is manifest in the other branches of the human race. Far from a desire to profit by their unique position and knowledge, or a desire to delve still further into the mystery, we find rather a tendency to return to idol worship and polytheism and even forms which are still lower. Indeed, the whole story of the Old Testament may well be summarized as the story of God through His servants fighting to preserve the knowledge of Himself among a recalcitrant people who were ever tending to lapse to the lower forms of religion. Not development, but definite retrogression. My point is that if this is true of these special people to whom God was constantly giving afresh definite and unique revelations and manifestations of Himself, it is obviously ridiculous to argue that the remainder of mankind was constantly seeking and striving for a fuller and yet fuller knowledge of God. Israel did not attain unto their belief in one God as the result of their own striving and effort. God revealed Himself to them in a unique manner. They did not seek God – they for ever wandered away from Him – He sought them and continued to guide them in spite of their waywardness. Biblical history, then, shows very clearly that the whole of mankind, which began with a knowledge of God and a life that corresponded, has fallen away from that knowledge, and that its tendency has been to sink lower and lower and further away from it. Man has not advanced from animism and fetishism, etc., to monotheism; he has degenerated in the opposite direction.

(ii) But this theory about man is also false to the history of man subsequent to biblical history. There is nothing which is more characteristic of the history of the Church than the strange periodicity which is to be found in her story. The history of the Church is in a sense a constant series of alternating periods of progress and decline, of spiritual revival and spiritual apathy. Without going any further, we can see this very clearly in the history of the Church in our own country. Were the doctrine of progress and development true, we would expect that each revival would lead to still further inevitable progress, that men having felt the stimulus and the impetus of a great time of blessing, would redouble their efforts and continue to grow and develop with an ever-increasing intensity. But such has not been the case. The fervour of the Protestant Reformation soon began to pass and to wane. Then came the Puritan period when the people of this country can be truly described as godly and God-fearing – one of the noblest periods in our history. But it soon gave way to the era of the Restoration with all its sin and shame. Who could believe that the England of the early part of the eighteenth century, as described for instance in the book, *England Before and After Wesley*, is the same country as the England of the Puritans? And so it has continued ever since. It is not only true of the country at large, but also of particular districts, of particular places of worship, and indeed of particular families and even of particular persons. Compare this country as she is today, and as she has become during the past twenty years, with the England of the mid-Victorian period.

(iii) 'But what of the evidence of comparative religion to which you have referred?' asks someone. We are very happy indeed to answer the question, for here, as in so many other realms, it is being discovered that the more thorough the research the more it confirms the biblical teaching. Nothing was more characteristic of the end of the Victorian era than the way in which theories were exalted into facts, and sweeping generalizations were made on the basis of very inadequate evidence without further confirmation and support. The tragedy is, of course, that once such ideas gain circulation, it takes a long time to undo their nefarious influence and effects. 'The man in the street' – yea, and at times in the colleges also – is often many years behind the latest discoveries. For the fact is that in the field of comparative religion the latest evidence definitely supports the Bible, and it is being acknowledged more and more by scholars of repute. Take, for instance, the following two passages from an article on the subject of Comparative Religion in the *Expository Times*, November, 1936: 'The first point brought out by the study of the most primitive cultures is the clear, vivid and direct belief in a Supreme Being which is found in them. This belief is to be found in a dominant position among all the primitive peoples. It must have been deeply rooted in this most ancient of human cultures at the very dawn of time, before the individual groups separated one from the other.' Again, 'The results of our study of the most primitive peoples, brief as it has been, seem to justify us in the conviction that religion began with the belief in a High God.' Likewise, Professor C. H. Dodd, in his commentary on the Epistle to the Romans, says, 'It is disputed among authorities on the comparative study of religion whether or not, in point of fact, idolatrous polytheism is a degeneration from an original monotheism of some kind; but at least there is a surprising amount of evidence that among very many peoples, not only in the higher civilizations of India and China, but in the barbarians of Central Africa and Australia, a belief in some kind of Creator Spirit subsists along with the superstitious cults of gods or demons, and often with a more or less obscure sense that this belief belongs to a superior, or a more ancient order.' (p.26, with reference to evidence given in Soderblom, *Das Werden des Gottesglaubens*). Then there is the truly monumental work of Father W. Schmidt (one of whose books is translated into English and bears the title of *The Origin of Religion*) which produces the most striking evidence to the same effect. In other words careful scientific investigation among the most primitive and backward races and tribes in the world produces evidence in that direction. Such a belief in the High God among such peoples is quite inexplicable apart from what we are told in the Bible. However far away they have wandered, and however low they may have sunk, there remains this memory and tradition of what was at the beginning the common knowledge of mankind.

(iv) But I would show you that this theory, quite apart from the evidence which I have adduced, is obviously false, were it merely from the standpoint of our knowledge of the nature of man. How utterly monstrous it is to postulate this idea of man as by nature imbued with this thirst and longing to know God when you look at modern man! According to the theory, we, living as we do today and with all our advantages of learning and understanding, and the great advantage of having at our disposal the result of the evidence of all who have gone before us, should be at the very top of the ladder. Our knowledge of God should be greater, and our desire for further knowledge should be still greater. Were it not tragic, it would be laughable to make such a suggestion. How easy it is to sit in a study and to evolve a theory arranging the evidence piece by piece on paper. Everything seems to fit in perfectly, and if it does not, with the complete freedom of the theorist, it is quite easy to manipulate and to rearrange. Thus men in their academic detachment have theorized about primitive tribes and savages. If they had but walked into the street or into the nightclubs of the West End, or into the hovels of the

East End, they would soon have found how false was their central hypothesis. It still remains true that 'the proper study of mankind is man.' What is true of the individual is true of all. What is true of each one of us is true of all. And the fact is that within ourselves is the final evidence which proves what St Paul says is true: there is in man this antagonism to God, 'the natural mind is enmity against God.' (Rom. 8:7) Man by nature always wants to break away and to get away from God, and St Paul tells us precisely and exactly why that is so and how that tendency shows itself.

It is due first to the inherent rebelliousness in man's nature, 'When they knew God they glorified Him not as God.' Men resent the very idea of God and feel that it means and implies that their liberty is somehow curtailed. They believe that they are fit to be 'masters of their fate and captains of their souls', and believing that, they demand the right to manage themselves in their own way and to live their own lives. They refuse to worship and to glorify God. They disown Him and turn their backs upon Him and say that they do not need Him. They renounce His way of life and shake off what they regard as the bondage and serfdom of religion and a life controlled by God. That is why man has always turned from God. He confuses lawlessness and licence with freedom; he is a rebel against God and refuses to glorify God.

But it is also due to a churlish element in man's nature. What else is an adequate description of what St Paul states in the words, 'Neither were thankful.' Were God merely a lawgiver we could in a sense understand man's rebellion against Him. But He is the 'giver of every good and perfect gift.' (James 1:17) He is 'the source and fount of every blessing.' Yet man spurns Him. At the very beginning, and in spite of the fact that God had placed him in the perfect conditions in Paradise, with everything that could be desired, man was ready to believe the base insinuation of Satan against God's character. He forgot all His goodness and kindness. And so it has continued. Observe it in the story of the Children of Israel. In spite of all God's patience with them, and His kindness to them, they constantly turned their backs upon Him. Nothing is so terrible in their record as their base ingratitude. But the crowning demonstration of this in the history of Israel, as in the history of mankind in general, is to be found in the rejection of Jesus Christ the Son of God. 'God so loved the world that He gave His only begotten Son.' Yea, gave Him to the cruel death on Calvary's hill that man might be pardoned and forgiven. But does mankind in general thank Him for so doing? Does it show and express its gratitude by surrendering itself to Him and trying to live to honour and glorify His name? Indeed, there is nothing that mankind so resents and hates as that crowning gift of God's love and mercy. 'The offence of the cross' (Gal. 5:11) is still the greatest offence in the Christian gospel. 'Neither were thankful.' If man objects to God's law, he objects still more to the truth that his salvation is entirely and solely dependent upon the grace and mercy of God.

And that is so, of course, for the reason expressed in St Paul's third step in this story of the decline and fall of mankind from the knowledge of God. It is man's pride. 'they became vain in their imagination (reasonings) and their foolish heart was darkened. Professing themselves to be wise, they became fools.' In other words, the final step is to reject God's revelation altogether and to substitute their own ideas and reasonings instead. They refuse the knowledge of God which is offered and given, they reject the wondrous works of God, but, feeling the need and the necessity of a religion, they proceed to make their own god or gods and then worship them and serve them. Man believes in his own mind and his own understanding, and the greatest insult that can ever be offered to him is to tell him, as Christ tells him, that he must become as a little child and be born again.

There, then, are the steps. We shall consider them again in greater detail in subsequent lectures. But there is the general picture. Man rebels against God as He is and as He reveals Himself. He even hates Him for His goodness. And then he proceeds to make his own gods. That was not only the story of mankind at the beginning, it is a precise and exact description of the past hundred years and especially of the past forty years. Whatever we may propose to do about our world, whatever plans and ideas we may have with regard to the future, if we ignore this basic fact all will be in vain. To be kind and to indulge in vague generalizations about man and his development, etc., and to invite him just as he is to follow Christ is not enough. Man must be convinced and convicted of his sin. He must face the naked, terrible truth about himself and his attitude towards God. It is only when he realizes that truth that he will be ready to believe the gospel and return to God.

That is the task of the Church; that is our task. Shall we commence upon it by examining ourselves? Do we accept the revelation of God as given in the Bible or do we base our views upon some human philosophy? Are we afraid of being called old-fashioned or out of date because we believe the Bible? Further, is God central and supreme in our lives, do we really glorify Him and show others that we are striving constantly to be well-pleasing in His sight? And, finally, are we doing all this gladly and willingly, not as people who are obeying a law but as men and women who, looking at the Son of God dying on the Cross on Calvary's hill for our sins, are so full of thankfulness and gratitude that we can gladly say:

'Love so amazing, so divine
Demands my soul, my life, my all.'

~ Chapter Two ~
Religion
and
Morality

~ Chapter Two ~
Religion
and
Morality

Romans 1:18

> 'For the wrath of God is revealed from heaven against all
> ungodliness and unrighteousness of men ...'

I propose to call your attention to but two words in the text
– namely, the words, 'ungodliness' and 'unrighteousness'.
And, in particular, we shall be interested in the order in
which the two words appear and the relationship between
them. To use more modern terms, we are invited by these
two words in our text, and the order in which they appear,
to consider the relationship between religion and morality.
Here again we are face to face with a matter which has
occupied much attention during the past hundred years. Here
also we are considering what can be termed another of the

fundamental fallacies with respect to life which are largely responsible for the present state of affairs in the world. And, precisely as we found to be the case in connection with the matter of comparative religion and man's approach to God, here again we find that during the past century there has been that same reversal of the condition which prevailed prior to that.

It is truly amazing and astonishing to note how this second half of the first chapter of the Epistle to the Romans sums up so perfectly the modern situation. Had it been written specially and specifically for our day it could not have been more perfect or more complete. Each of the main trends in the thought and reasoning of the majority of people is considered carefully, and traced to its ultimate consequences.

The key to the understanding of the whole situation is in the realization of the fact that man by nature is inimical to God, and does his utmost to get rid of God and what he regards as the incubus of revealed religion. Man, rebelling against God as He has revealed Himself and from the kind of life that God dictates, proceeds to make for himself new gods, and new religions, and to elaborate a new way of life and of salvation.

Here, in this special matter that we propose to consider together, we have a perfect example and illustration of that tendency.

Until about a hundred years ago it was true to say of the vast majority of the people of this country that religion came first and that morality and ethics followed. In other words, all their thinking about the good life, religion and their understanding of the teaching of the Bible. The fear of God' was the controlling motive; it was, to use the language of the Old Testament, the beginning of wisdom. This was so, of course, because it was as the result of the various religious revivals and movements that the people had been awakened to a realization of the utter sinfulness and depravity of their lives. As the result of becoming religious they had seen the importance of right living. That was the position.

But then came the great change. At first it was not an open denial of God, but a change and a reversal in the emphasis which was placed on these two matters. More and more, interest became fixed upon ethics, and the emphasis was placed increasingly on morality at the expense of religion. God was not denied, but was relegated increasingly to the position of a mere background to life. All this was done on the plea and the pretext that formerly too much emphasis had been placed upon the personal and experiential aspect of religion, and that the ethical and social aspects had not been emphasized sufficiently. But increasingly the position developed into one in which it was stated, quite openly and unashamedly, that really nothing mattered but morality and conduct. Religion was seriously discounted, and it was even stated blatantly that nothing mattered save that one should live the good life and do one's best. Everything that stressed the miraculous intervention of God in life, and for man's salvation, was queried and then denied; everything that emphasized the vital link between God and man was minimized until it became almost non-existent. Creeds and confessions of faith, the sacraments, and even attendance at all in a place of worship, were all regarded as expedients which had served a useful purpose in the past, while men were ignorant, and had to be more or less frightened into living the good life. They were now no longer necessary. Jesus of Nazareth, far from being the unique Son of God who had come on earth in order to prepare a miraculous way of salvation for men, was but the greatest moral teacher and exemplar of all time – simply greater than all others, not essentially different. The religious motive and the religious background to the good life practically disappeared altogether, and their place was taken by education and a belief in the inevitably good effects of acts of social amelioration. With an air of great patronage and condescension we were told that the magic and the rites and the taboos of religion had been more or less necessary in the past, but that now man, in his intelligent and intellectual modern condition, had no need of such things. Indeed they had become insulting. Nothing was necessary save that man should be shown what was good and given instruction concerning it.

Has that not been the popular teaching? The supreme thing has been to live the good life, to be moral. The majority have ceased to attend a place of worship at all, and (alas!) many who do attend, do so, not because they believe it to be essential and vital, but rather out of habit or because they believe vaguely that it is somehow the right thing to do. Religion far from being the mainspring and source of all ideas concerning life and how it should be lived, has become a mere appendage even in the case of many who still adhere to it. Righteousness, or morality, has been exalted to the supreme position, and little is heard of godliness. Like the Pharisees of old, there have been many amongst us who were shocked and scandalized by certain acts of unrighteousness, but who failed to realize that their own self-righteousness denoted an ungodliness which was infinitely more reprehensible in the eyes of God. The order has been reversed: morality has taken precedence over religion, unrighteousness is regarded as a more heinous crime than ungodliness.

But now we must come to the vital question. What has been the result of all this? To what consequences has it led? The answer is to be found in the present state of the world. We were told that man could be trained not to sin. He could be educated into seeing the folly of war. And here we are in the midst of a war. But apart from the war, and prior to it, this teaching had led to the terrible moral muddle that characterized the life of the people of this country and most other countries. The very term 'moral' has been evacuated almost entirely of any meaning, and the sins of the past have become 'the thing to do' of the present. No one, surely, can deny the statement that, morally and intellectually, the masses of the people have sunk to a lower level than at any time during the past two hundred years, in fact since the evangelical revival of the eighteenth century.

Now, my whole case is that that, according to the Bible, is something which is quite inevitable, something which follows as the night the day. Once the relative positions of religion and morality are reversed from what we find in our text, the inevitable result is what we find stated in such clear and terrible terms in the remainder of this chapter. Religion must precede morality if morality itself

is to survive. Godliness is essential to ethics. Nothing but
a belief in God and a desire to glorify Him, based upon
our realization of our utter dependence upon Him and our
acceptance of His way of life and salvation in Jesus Christ
His Son, can ever lead to a good society. This is not merely
a dogmatic statement. It can be proved and demonstrated
repeatedly in the history of mankind. As St Paul reminds us
here, it is the essential story of mankind. Observe it in the
story of the Children of Israel in the Old Testament. See it
again in the history of Greece and Rome. They had exalted
moral ideas and fine ethical systems and conceptions of
law and justice, but the ultimate downfall of both is to be
traced finally to moral degeneracy. And then consider the
history of this country. Religion and spiritual revival have
always led to moral and intellectual awakening and a desire
to produce a better society. And conversely, ungodliness
has always led to unrighteousness. A slackening in spiritual
zeal and fervour, even though the zeal and fervour be
transferred to a desire to improve the state of society, has
always eventuated ultimately in both moral and intellectual
decline. The great periods in the history of this country
in every sphere are the Elizabethan, the Puritan and the
Victorian. Each followed a striking religious revival. But
as religion was allowed to sink into the background, and
even into oblivion, and men thought that they could live by
morality alone, degeneration set in rapidly. Emil Brunner
has said that this is so definite as to be capable of statement
as a law of life in which there are distinct steps and stages.
He puts it thus: 'The feeling for the personal and the human
which is the fruit of faith may outlive for a time the death of

the roots from which it has grown, but this cannot last very long. As a rule the decay of religion works out in the second generation as moral rigidity, and in the third generation as the breakdown of all morality. Humanity without religion has never been a historical force capable of resistance. Even today, severance from the Christian faith, whenever it has been of some duration, works out in the dehumanization of all human conditions. "The wine of life has been poured out"; the dregs alone remain.'

Here, then, is a fundamental principle which we must grasp firmly before we begin to organize a new state of society and a new world. Religion, a true belief in God in Jesus Christ, is fundamental, vital, essential. Any attempt to organize society without that basis is doomed to failure even as it always has been in the past. The pragmatic test, as we have just seen, demonstrates that abundantly. But we are not left merely in the world of pragmatism. A study of the Bible, indeed a study of man himself in the light of the Bible, furnishes us with many reasons which explain why it must inevitably be the case that to trust to morality alone without religion, or to place morality before religion, leads only to eventual disaster. We must consider some of these reasons.

(i) First of all we note that to do so is an insult to God. We must start with this because here we have the real explanation of all that follows. But even apart from that we must start with this because it is absolute. And we must be very careful always to draw that distinction. Before we begin to think about ourselves and the result in ourselves, before we begin to consider the good of society or anything else, we must start with God and we must start by worshipping God. If we advocate godliness simply because it leads to the true morality, if we commend religion because it leads to the best state of society, then we are again reversing the order actually and insulting God. God must never be regarded as a means to an end; and religion is not to be commended primarily because of certain benefits which follow its practice. And yet one hears statements not at all infrequently which give the impression that religion and the Bible are to be valued solely in terms of England's greatness. That is why the charge of national hypocrisy is so frequently levelled against us by other nations. We tend to believe, and perhaps rightly, that we have been blessed in the past because we have been religious. But when we make use of that fact and advocate religion in order that we may be blessed we are insulting God. The more religious the nation, the more moral and the more dependable and solid is the nation. Hence the temptation to statesmen and leaders to pay lip service to religion, and to believe in its maintenance in a general form. But that is the very opposite of what I would stress, and what is emphasized everywhere in the Bible. God is to be worshipped because He is God, because He is the Creator, because He is the Almighty, because He is the 'high and lofty One that inhabiteth eternity,' because His Name is Holy. And in His presence it is impossible to think of anything else. All thoughts of self and of benefits that may accrue, all ideas concerning the possible results and advantages to ourselves, or to our class or country, are banished. He is supreme and He is alone. To place anything before God is to deny Him, however noble and exalted that thing may be. The results and blessings of salvation, the moral life and the improved state of society – all these things are the consequents of true belief and they must never be allowed to usurp the supreme position. Indeed, as I have said, if we truly worship God and realize His presence, they cannot do so.

This is one of the most subtle dangers that faces us as we try to think out and plan a new state of society for the future. It is a danger which can be seen in the writings of a number of writers today who are concerned about the state of this country. I think in particular of men like Mr T. S. Eliot and Mr Middleton Murray. They advocate a religious society and a Christian education – or what they call such – simply because they have found all else to fail, and because they think that this is more likely to be successful. But they fail to realize that before you can have a Christian society and Christian education you must first of all have Christians. No education or culture, no mode of training, will ever produce Christians and the corresponding morality. To do that we must come face to face with God and see our sin and helpless plight; we must know something about the wrath of God, and repent before Him and then receive His gracious offer of salvation in Jesus Christ His Son. But that is not mentioned. Men ever desire the benefits of Christianity without paying the price. They need to be reminded again that 'God is not mocked,' and that even in the name of Christian civilization He is often grievously insulted. Whatever may follow, God must be worshipped for His own sake because He is God. He demands it and will have it.

(ii) But, secondly, I would show you that to place morality before religion is also to insult man. It is remarkable to note how it invariably happens that when man sets out to exalt himself, he always ends by lowering himself and insulting himself. This is something which we hope to consider again in greater detail. I am anxious to emphasize the principle now. Verse 22 sums it up very perfectly by telling us that 'professing themselves to be wise they became fools.' Man always feels that God fetters him and refuses to allow him to give free scope to his wonderful powers and capacities. He rebels against God in order to exert himself and to express himself – he rebels in the name of freedom, proposing to produce a larger and nobler type of personality. That, as we have seen, has been the real meaning of the revolt against revealed religion during the past hundred years. Ah! how much we have heard about the emancipation of man! Moral man was conceived to be so much higher than religious man. That was why morality was placed before religion. But what are the actual facts? Let me but cite them in order that I may demonstrate that the old rule is still in force, and that man in attempting to elevate himself has simply succeeded in insulting himself.

For one thing, morality is interested in a man's actions rather than in the man himself. At the very outset it hurls that insult at us. I do not pause to emphasize the point that its interest in our very actions is always much more negative than positive, which makes the insult still greater. But regarding it at its very best and highest and at its most positive, nothing is so insulting to personality than to say that its actions alone matter. There is no need to demonstrate this point. We have but to recollect what we think of the kind of person who shows clearly that he is not really interested in us at all, but simply in what we do or what we are — our office or status, or position, or the possibility of our being of some help or value to him. How insulting! But that is precisely the position with respect to morality. It is interested only in our conduct and behaviour. It may argue that as our conduct improves, so we improve. But that does not lessen the insult, for it leaves me, the essential 'I' who I am, still subservient to my conduct. And that is ultimately destructive of personality. How evident that has become in these last few years. We have all become standardized in almost every respect, and there is a monotonous drab sameness about the whole of life. As we have concentrated more and more on conduct and behaviour, on the mere acquisition of knowledge and how we appear before others, not only has variety vanished, but genius and 'character' have become rarer and rarer, and true individuality has been lost.

But again, morality is always more interested in man's associations than in man himself. Its interest is in society, or the state, or the group, and its main concern about the individual is simply that he should be brought or made to conform to a common pattern. Its very terms prove that: 'state,' 'society,' 'social'; those are its words. The individual personality has been ignored and forgotten. Everything is done for the good of the state or of society. Here again the argument is, that as the mass is improved, so will the individual be improved. But that is to insult personality by suggesting that it is merely a speck in a huge mass of humanity. Religion believes in improving society by improving the individuals that compose it. Morality believes in improving the individual by improving the general state. I leave you to decide which really places value on the human personality, on man as such. And the methods employed show this still more clearly. Morality uses compulsion. It legislates and forces men to conform to the general standard. Whether we will or not, we have to do certain things. That this is essential to govern a state, I grant freely, but still I argue that it is essentially insulting to personality. Moreover, it is the very antithesis of Christianity, which brings a man to see the rightness of the thing advocated, and creates within him a deep longing and desire to exemplify it in his life. Morality dictates and commands, but as St Paul tells the Galatians, 'faith worketh by love' (Gal. 5:6).

But above all else, morality insults man by taking no account whatsoever of that which is highest in man, of that which ultimately differentiates man from the animal. I refer to his relationship with God. It deals with him only on the lower planes and forgets that he was made for God. At its best and highest it sets limits to his achievements, and to the possibilities of his nature. It may help to make man a noble and a thinking animal, but it knows nothing of the glorious possibility of man becoming a son of God. It is earthbound and temporal, and entirely ignorant of the delectable mountains and the vision of eternity. And it ultimately fails for that reason. A simple and familiar illustration may help here: a little child is away from home, perhaps even staying with relatives. He becomes homesick and cries for his mother. The friends do their best. They produce toys, they suggest games, they offer sweets and chocolates and everything they know the child enjoys. But it all avails nothing. Dolls and toys and

44

the rarest delicacies cannot satisfy when a child wants his mother. They are flung contemptuously aside by a young philosopher who realizes that, at that point, they are a veritable insult. He needs his mother and nothing else will do. Man in his state of sin does not know what he really needs. But he shows very clearly that the best and highest offers of men cannot satisfy him. Deep within him there is that profound dissatisfaction which can be satisfied by nothing less than God Himself. Failure to realize this is not only inadequate, it is insulting. Man was made for God, and in the image of God, and though he has sinned and fallen and wandered far away, there is still within him that nostalgia which can never be satisfied until he returns home and to his Father.

(iii) But, thirdly, this attempt to give morality priority over religion also fails because it provides no ultimate authority or sanction for man's life. Here we are coming to the realm of the practical application of all we have said hitherto. We are urged to live the good life. But immediately the question arises, 'Why should we live the good life?' And, here, face to face with this question of 'Why?' this isolation of morality from religion leads again to failure. We can show this along two main lines.

The view that regards morality as an end in itself and which advocates it for its own sake only, bases its answer to this question 'Why?' upon the intellect alone. It appeals to our reason and to our understanding. What was formerly regarded as sin it regards as due to nothing but ignorance or lack of true education. It sets out, therefore, to show and to picture a higher and a better type of life. It outlines its

Utopia, in which all people being taught and educated will restrain themselves and do their utmost to contribute to the common good. It shows the evil results and consequences of certain actions both to the individual himself, and also to the community at large. But, further, it will have him see that such actions are quite unworthy of him, and that in committing them he is lowering his own standard and being unworthy of his own essential self. That is its method. It teaches man about his own wonderful nature and of how he has developed from the animal. It pleads with him to see that he must now leave the animal behind and rise to the heights of his own development. It then tries to charm him into an acceptance of these views by holding before him pictures of the ideal society. It is essentially an appeal to the intellect, to the reason, to the rational side of man's nature.

But this means that ultimately it is a matter of opinion. It claims that its view is the highest, the best, and also leads to the greatest happiness. But when it meets with those who say that they disagree and that in their view it fails to cater for man's real nature, it has nothing to say by way of reply. And that has been the position increasingly, especially since the last war, with the cult of self-expression becoming stronger and stronger, and ever more popular. Those who belong to this cult have denied that the picture drawn by the moralists is the best and highest. They have regarded it rather as something that fetters and restrains, something therefore which is inimical to the highest interest of the self. Placing happiness and pleasure as the supreme desiderata they have drawn up a scheme for life and for conduct which is the exact opposite. We have no time to consider that now. All I am concerned to show is that, face to face with that challenge, any moral system which is not based upon religion has no answer. One opinion is as good as another, and therefore any man can do as he likes. There is no ultimate authority.

But this can be shown also in another way. The basing of the appeal solely upon the intellect and the rational part of man's nature is also doomed to failure because it ignores what is most vital in man. That has been the real fallacy behind most thinking during the past century. Man was regarded as intellect and reason alone. He had but to be told what was right and how he would do it. It is extraordinary to note how this view has prevailed in spite of the glaring facts to the contrary. The possession of intellect does not guarantee a moral life, as the newspapers and the biographies and memoirs constantly testify. An educated and cultured man does not always and inevitably lead a good life. Those who know most about the consequences of certain sins against the body, are often those who fall most frequently into those sins. Why is this? Here the new psychology has certainly given valuable aid, and it is astonishing that its evidence has not finally exploded that view of life which regards man as intellect alone. Within man there are deep primal instincts. He is a creature of desire and lust. His brain is not an independent isolated machine, his will does not exist in a state of complete detachment. These other forces are constantly exerting themselves, and constantly influencing the higher powers. A man therefore may know that a certain course of action is wrong, but that does not matter. He desires that thing, and his desire can be so strong that he can even rationalize it and produce arguments in its favour. But you remember how St Paul, in the seventh chapter of the Epistle to the Romans, has put it all so perfectly: 'For what which I do I allow not: for what I would, that do I not; but that I hate, that do I.' (v. 15) a view which fails to realize that that is fundamental to human nature is of necessity doomed to failure. Man being what he is needs a higher sanction. Appeals to reason and to the will are not enough. The whole man must be included, and especially the element of desire.

(iv) But, lastly, we must say just a word on the other vital practical aspect of this matter. Having asked the question why one should lead the good life, the further question arises, 'How am I to lead the good life?' And here once more we find that morality without religion entirely fails because it provides no power. 'For the good that I would I do not: but the evil which I would not that I do,' says St Paul (v. 19). That is the problem. The lack of power, the failure to do what we know we ought to do or what we would like to do, and the corresponding failure not to do what we know to be wrong. Mankind needs not only knowledge of the truth but, still more, power. Here morality fails, for it leaves the problem in our hands. We have to do everything. But, as we have just seen, that, in a sense, is the whole of our problem. We cannot. We fail. Ultimately moral systems only appeal to and help a certain type of person. If we are what is called 'naturally good' and naturally interested in such things, they may help us much and encourage us. And when I say 'naturally good' I mean good in the sight of man,

not of God, good in the sense of not being guilty of certain
sins, not good in the sense of the biblical terms righteous and
holy. Such people are helped by moral systems. But what of
those who are not constituted in that way? What of those
who are natural rebels, those who are more dynamic and
full of life? Those to whom wrong and evil come more easily
and naturally than good? Clearly morality cannot help, for
it leaves us precisely and exactly what and where we were.
It provides us with no power to restrain ourselves from sin,
for its arguments can be easily brushed aside. It provides
no power to restore us when we have fallen into sin. It
leaves us as condemned failures and, indeed, makes us feel
hopeless. It reminds us that we have failed, that we have
been defeated, that we have not maintained the standard.
And even if it appeals to us to try again it really condemns
us while so doing and dooms us to failure. For it still leaves
the problem to us. It cannot help us. It has no power to give
us. And having failed once, we argue, we are likely to fail
again. Why try, therefore? Let us give in and give up and
abandon ourselves to our fate. And alas! How many have
done so and for that very reason?

And in the same way it has no enabling power to give us.
It provides a standard, but it does not help us to attain unto
it. It is really nothing but good advice. It gives no power.

We have seen, therefore, that it fails in every respect,
theoretical and practical.

How tragic it is that mankind should so long have been
guilty of this foolish error of reversing the true order of
religion and morality! For once they are placed in their
right positions the situation is entirely changed. In precisely

the same way as morality alone fails, the gospel of Christ succeeds. It starts with God and exists to glorify His holy Name. It restores man into the right relationship to Him, reconciling him to God through the blood of Christ. It tells man that he is more important than his own actions or his environment, and that when he is put right, he must then proceed to put them right. It caters for the whole man, body, soul, and spirit, intellect, desire and will, by giving him the most exalted view of all, and filling him with a passion and a desire to live the good life in order to express his gratitude to God for His amazing love. And it provides him with power. In the depth of his shame and misery as the result of his sin and failure, it restores him by assuring him that Christ has died for him and his sins, and that God has forgiven him. It calls him to a new life and a new start, promising him power that will overcome sin and temptation, and will at the same time enable him to live the life he believes and knows he ought to live.

There, and there alone, lies the only hope for men and for the world. Everything else has been tried and has failed. Ungodliness is the greatest and the central sin. It is the cause of all our other troubles. Men must return to God and start with Him. And, God be praised, the way for them to do so is still wide open in 'Jesus Christ and Him crucified' (1 Cor. 2:2).

~ Chapter Three ~

The
Nature
of
Sin

~ Chapter Three ~
The
Nature of Sin

Romans 1: 18, 28 and 32

18. 'For the wrath of God is revealed from heaven against all ungodliness and unrighteousness of men, who hold the truth in unrighteousness;'

28. 'And even as they did not like to retain God in their knowledge, God gave them over to a reprobate mind, to do those things which are not convenient;'

32. 'Who knowing the judgment of God, that they which commit such things are worthy of death, not only do the same, but have pleasure in them that do them.'

I select these three particular verses from this section in order that we may consider the whole question of sin, at least as to its essential nature. We are driven to this in our study of this section by a kind of logical necessity. We have seen that man by nature is opposed to God and not a being who desires God. And we have seen that mere proposals and schemes for moral reform are not sufficient to deal with the problem of mankind. Why is this? What is it in human nature that accounts for this? These questions cannot be raised without our finding ourselves at once face to face with the doctrine of sin.

Of this doctrine we can safely say that it is one of the most hotly contested of all the doctrines. This is not at all surprising, for it is in many ways the very crux of the whole problem of man. There is certainly no subject which calls, and has called, forth so much scorn and sarcasm and derision. There has been no doctrine which has been so ridiculed. There is none which calls forth such passion and hatred. That, I say, is not at all surprising, for at any rate two very definite reasons. One is that if the Christian doctrine of sin is right and true, then the very basis of the modern doctrine of man is entirely destroyed. And in the same way this doctrine of sin is the essential postulate which leads to and demands the whole scheme of miraculous and supernatural salvation which is outlined in the Bible. It is not surprising, therefore, that the battle has been severest and hottest just at this point.

Here again, as we consider this matter, we find exactly, and precisely as we have done on former occasions, that the movement of thought has followed certain definite steps. And again as before, the main thing we notice is that the idea concerning sin which has been most popular during the past hundred years has been the exact opposite of that which obtained previously. Whatever else we may say about these modern ideas, we have to grant that they are consistent with each other. They all belong to a definite pattern and are parts of a general scheme.

The central idea is the profound change in the view of man as a being, his nature, his origin, his development, etc. A modern writer puts all this perfectly in one phrase when he said that the future historians of the past hundred years would probably not fail to observe that the decline, and the disappearance, of the doctrine of sin followed a parallel course to the doctrine of the evolution of man from the animal. That is the basic position. The new view of man at the centre had of necessity to lead to corresponding changes in the views held of man's activities. Nowhere does that appear more clearly than in this question of sin.

The modern theory was not foolish enough to say that there was nothing wrong with man or that he was perfect. His actions alone proved that such was not the case. He still did things that he should not do, things that were opposed to his own interests and to the interests of society. He also failed to live the kind of life they believed he should live. All these facts in personal life, and further facts, such as war, in connection with communal life had to be faced and had to be accounted for somehow. Now it is just there that the change was introduced. The facts were not denied. But when it became a question of evaluating the facts and of explaining the origin of these facts, the new view was an entire departure from that which had obtained previously. The old view, as we shall see later in greater detail, had held that sin was deliberate, that it was something which had entered into human life, causing it to fall and creating a new problem. It stated that man had started in a state of perfection, and that sin was that which, entering in, had caused him to fall from that state. But the new view regarding man as a creature that has developed and evolved out of the animal, obviously could not subscribe to that old view and explanation of man's faults and failures. And it has resolutely refused to do so. It provides, therefore, its own theory and supposed explanation.

We cannot consider this in detail, but we must note some of the commoner expressions of this view. Some of them are highly philosophical, while others are more practical. Belonging to the former category is the view that describes what has been called sin as a principle of necessary antagonism which seems to be a part of life. Sin is not so much evil as a kind of resistance which is provided by life in order that the positive faculties may be exercised and developed. Sin can be regarded as dumb-bells which have to be lifted in order to develop the intellectual and moral muscles, or as a resistance which has to be removed in order that we may progress. It is something essential to growth and on the whole good rather than bad.

Another view regards sin as the opposition of the lower propensities to a gradually developing moral consciousness. Here again the view is not that sin is actually evil or wrong, but that it is the fight put up by our lingering animal instincts against the demands made by our dawning and ever increasing moral consciousness. It is the struggle, if you like, between the man in us and the animal in us. Not that the animal is bad *per se*, but that it only becomes bad if we allow it to preponderate in our lives when the strictly human should be in control.

Another view puts that in a slightly different way by saying that sin is a kind of negative state, a negation rather than something positive and actual. It is the lack of positive qualities, lack of their full development. It is not so much an activity on the part of the lower, as a failure of the higher to exert themselves as they should. Thus we should not say that a man is actually bad; we should say that he is not good. Sin is a negative condition, a negation.

And then there is the view that regards it as almost entirely a matter of knowledge and of education. If, it argues, the lower is overexerting itself and the higher is not playing its part as it should, it is clear that the reason for this is lack of knowledge, lack of training, lack of education. This may well be due to the environment in which the man has been brought up. This is the view, therefore, that regards sin as being primarily a matter of housing and of education and which advocates slum clearance schemes and educational systems as the one and only necessary cure for the problem.

There are other views that we need not mention, such as the view which refuses to grant anything wrong at all in what is called sin. But there we have the main views. And it is clear that they all belong to the same pattern and are all based on the same central idea. That central idea we can state in this form. According to this view sin is not really a serious problem at all. The fathers, we are told, hopelessly exaggerated it, and not only made themselves miserable and unhappy, but also all others who came under their influence. The old view, we are told, led to endless morbidity and introspection and often even to despair. By making too much of the problem, it increased and magnified it instead of regarding it quietly as but an inevitable stage in man's evolution. What was really nothing but a kind of spiritual growing pains was exaggerated into a dread disease, and one of the natural adjustments in connection with the physiological process and development of life was regarded as a pathological condition. The whole of life thus became sombre and dull, and men lived in a state of bondage and slavery. But the modern idea is entirely different.

In the same way, the new view refuses to regard sin as an active force and power, as something which has an independent existence apart from man. It is rather the failure to learn as we should about goodness, beauty and truth. It is a mere relic, a mere negative phase. It is not something in and of itself. It is just that stage of immaturity where the child has not yet become the man, or where the animal has not yet become entirely human.

And the other characteristic of this view is that it does not regard man as really responsible himself – it is always the conditions and surroundings or the opportunities that the man has had. The responsibility is taken from man and is placed in his economic conditions, or his home life, or early upbringing, and indeed at times in his physical make-up. The failure is to be pitied only. He is not to be blamed, he is not to be punished. We must speak nicely to him and encourage him to be nice and decent, whether he is an individual or a nation, like modern Germany. (There, incidentally, is a perfect illustration of this whole attitude. It is seen in the case of those who regard Germany as innocent, and who blame the Treaty of Versailles for all our present troubles.) But, clearly, the most significant fact concerning the modern view is that it makes no mention at all of sin in the sight of God. It never uses the word guilt and is quite unaware of the fact that sin is primarily transgression.

Now, the biblical view of sin is the precise opposite of this at every point. Let us but summarize it. It starts by saying that sin is not to be explained merely as a part of the process in man's development. For sin is something that is outside man, something which can exist and which does exist apart from man. It is something that has entered human nature from without. No view therefore which regards it in purely human terms can possibly be adequate or sufficient. This it explains further by showing how actual experience points that way. We are aware of a power other than ourselves acting upon us, and influencing us, a power with which we can struggle and fight, a power which we can overcome and dismiss. This is seen supremely, of course, in the temptation of our Lord. No temptation could or did arise within Him, or from His nature, because He was perfect. The temptation, the incitement to sin, was entirely external.

But it is not enough just to say that sin is a power that has independent existence. It is a mighty power, a terrible power. It has a fiendish quality, a malignity which is truly terrifying. It is a definite spirit, a positive attitude, active and powerful. Furthermore, it is a power that man has allowed to enter his life and which affects him profoundly and vitally. It is not something light and comparatively trivial. It does not belong to the order of vestigial remains. It does not merely affect one part of man and his nature. It is so deep-seated and so much a part of us that the entire man is affected – the intellect, the desires and therefore the will. Indeed, it constitutes such a terrible problem that God alone in Christ can deal with it.

Now, it is scarcely necessary to indicate that it is vitally important that we should be clear as to which of these two views is correct, before we begin to plan for the future. Can we regard this problem lightly, and can we be optimistic in our view of man and of life? Is what we call 'sin' something which mankind as it continues to progress will gradually slough off and leave behind it? Will the lower and the animal of necessity deteriorate and decay, and the higher and the human inevitably continue to develop and to increase? The answers to these questions are all important. We could in a sense answer them by just making an analysis of the history of the past century, when the optimistic view came into vogue, and during which its principles have been put into practice educationally, socially, and in almost every department of life. That analysis would reveal the utter fallacy of that light view of sin. Indeed, the condition of the world at this hour is a sufficient answer in and of itself. But we refrain from stating our answer in that way for two reasons. One is that the optimistic temperament and outlook are rarely influenced by facts. Like Mr Micawber, when all its schemes go wrong, and all its optimistic prophecies and

60

predictions are falsified by events, it still retains its serenity, it still waits for what it has envisaged to 'turn up'. Were this not the case, the last war and its consequences would have been sufficient. But in spite of the glaring facts to the contrary the exponents of that view clung tenaciously to it. My second reason for not adopting that method is that it is always better to deal with the principles that underlie conduct and actions. If it can be shown that the principles are wrong, then clearly what emanates from them must be wrong. And in any case the trouble with the life of sin, according to the Bible, is not merely that it leads to disastrous results, but that it is wrong in and of itself and in its very nature and essence.

We propose therefore to consider positively what the Apostle has to say on this subject in the verses we are considering. Never, perhaps, has there been a more thorough and terrifying analysis of sin and all its ways. And yet how masterly it is. The Apostle shrinks from nothing. He states the truth baldly and yet with such economy of style and language that he never becomes sensational. He feels he must reveal the whole horrible business in all its fullness and entirety, lest any illusions concerning it might remain; but not for a moment does he pander to the depraved taste of those who would like to wallow in the mire of the unsavoury details. What a contrast to the type of novel and of literature that has been so popular during the past years. God grant that as we try to unfold His teaching we also may be enabled to observe the same carefulness.

What Paul has to say about sin can be considered most conveniently under three main headings.

(i) His first great principle is that sin is deliberate. In the eighteenth verse he turns from the glorious proclamation of the gospel to the other side of the picture. He reminds them that as the righteousness of God is revealed from faith to faith, so also 'the wrath of God is revealed from heaven against all ungodliness and unrighteousness of men.' And at once he begins to attack sin at the very centre. 'The wrath is revealed,' he says, 'against all ungodliness and unrighteousness of men, who hold down the truth in unrighteousness.' At once he levels against sin the charge of deliberateness. But he repeats it in verse 28, where he says, 'And even as they did not like to retain God in their knowledge,' or, as the **RV** has it, 'and even as they refused to have God in their knowledge,' or, as the margin has it, 'even as they did not approve of God,' God 'gave them over to a reprobate mind.' Still the same charge. And once more in the last verse (32): 'Who knowing the judgment of God, that they which commit such things are worthy of death, not only do the same, but have pleasure in them that do them.'

These three statements show us the essential nature of sin and especially the element of deliberateness. How far removed they are from that other picture of men which represents them as more sinned against than sinning owing to their circumstances and surroundings, or as creatures who are in a negative stage of their existence! How far removed from the idea that says that sin is not positive, but rather a failure to attain to the true level! Or that sin is due merely to lack of knowledge and of training! For the fact is that it is altogether and entirely positive. It is something active and militant. St Paul suggests, if we take the verses in the following order, 28, 32 and 18, that there are at least three stages in the manifestation of the activity.

The first is that men do not like to retain God in their knowledge, or refuse to have God in their knowledge. Having started with that knowledge, they decide that they are not going to continue in it. They do not approve of the knowledge. It is not simply that they fail to attain to its standard; they deliberately reject it as a standard. It is not only that they miss the mark; they cease to aim at the mark at all, and refuse to recognize it as a standard and objective in life. God is deliberately dethroned and His entire way of life is jettisoned. As that was true in the early days of the story of mankind, it has been true of recent times. There was in this country a religious background and a religious tradition. There was a view of life and a way of life based upon belief in God. It is a view which is still known to most people, a view with which all have come in contact at some time or other. It is a view, therefore, which has to be deliberately rejected before men can live the kind of life which so many are living today. They decide that it is wrong or foolish or old-fashioned, and, knowing precisely and exactly what they are doing, they reject it and choose its very antithesis. Indeed, the vast majority not only do not deny this, but actually glory in the fact that they have done so.

This is further shown by the fact that though they know what the Scripture teaches about God's view of such conduct, they not only do so, but delight in all others who do likewise. What proves so conclusively that evil and wrongdoing are not mere negative remains of the animal part of our nature is the fact that in spite of all warnings of consequences, and, at all costs, man persists in sinning. Though it may mean loss of health or loss of money, though it involves loss of character and lowering of standard, and even though it threatens to affect eternal destiny, still men persist in it. What is worse is the pleasure which they take in the thing itself, the way they enjoy it, and talk and joke about it. Were it the case that they were ashamed, the argument about the negative nature of sin might at least have a semblance of truth, but the fact is that men boast of their sins and talk about them and encourage others to do precisely the same. One has but to read the newspapers or to listen to the wireless to discover how true this has become of life.

But the third step is that which the Apostle describes by saying that they 'hold down' the truth in unrighteousness. This is the final and clearest proof of the activity of sin and its deliberate character. Though men decide not to believe in God and to put Him and His ways out of their lives, though they ignore all consequences and in a spirit of bravado decide to follow the other life, they do not therefore finish with God and truth at that point. The truth continues to remind them of its existence and to worry them. It does so most definitely, of course, in and through the conscience. It warns, it condemns, and it prohibits. The Truth is not static and lifeless. It is actually within us – there is 'the light that lighteth every man that cometh into the world'. That is the whole meaning of remorse and what we call the pangs of conscience. These become particularly marked at certain times – for example, illness or death or war, etc..The Truth follows us and worries us. Man is not ignorant. He knows the difference between good and evil, right and wrong. This knowledge confronts him always and worries him. But what he does about it, says Paul, is to hold it down, to suppress it, to do his utmost to stifle it, and to destroy it. Men try to throttle this activity of truth within themselves. The ways in which they do so are almost endless. They argue against the truth and try to explain it away. They deny its postulates and try to rationalize their own misdeeds. They would even try to explain away conscience itself in terms of psychology. Anything to silence its voice and to rid themselves of its condemnations. And when argument and denial and persuasion are of no avail men deliberately plunge still further into sin, hoping thereby to drown it. They refuse deliberately to give themselves time to think and to reason; they deliberately avoid the truth and do their utmost to conceal it from themselves. 'Why stop?' they ask. 'Why think when thinking is painful and disconcerting?' Thus they hold down the truth in the interest of their unrighteousness and by means of it. The trouble with mankind is not that it does not know enough about the truth. It deliberately denies the truth. Its difficulty is not that its advance in the direction of truth is somewhat slow and laboured. It prefers to go in the opposite direction. Its problem is not that it lacks sufficient light, but rather, as we are reminded in John 3:19, that 'men loved darkness rather than light because their deeds were evil'.

(ii) But St Paul is also anxious to show that sin is debasing and depraves. This we see most clearly in verses 21-23 and verse 25, where he sums up it all by saying, 'who changed the truth of God into a lie, and worshipped and served the creature more than the Creator, who is blessed for ever. Amen.' His case is, as we have seen, that men give up the worshipping of God deliberately and that therefore they are inexcusable. But that is not all. There is something else which is quite as characteristic of sin and its effects and which arouses the Apostle's anger. Were men to give up God and then remain irreligious and cease to worship altogether, the situation would be bad enough. But actually it is worse than that. For sin is not only deliberate, but also debasing in its effects and essentially depraved in its nature. Having given up God, men do not cease to be religious, they do not cease to worship. They make other gods for themselves and then proceed to worship them. What is the nature of the new gods? Paul does not give the complete list; that, in a sense, would be impossible, for they are so many. But he gives a glimpse into the condition of heathendom in the words, 'they changed the glory of the uncorruptible God into an image made like to corruptible man, and to birds, and fourfooted beasts, and creeping things.' And again 'and worshipped and served the creature more than the Creator'. So he summarizes all the phenomena of paganism, with its worship of ancestors, sun, moon, stars, four-footed beasts, birds, trees, stones, its belief in magic, etc.. From the glory of the uncorruptible God to – such things! From the Creator to the creature. Comment is scarcely necessary. What a fall! What a lowering of the standard! How utterly debased!

But what calls forth the sarcasm of Paul is that all this was done in the name of wisdom! They preened and prided themselves on it and boasted of their advance. What can account for this? Surely there is no adequate explanation save that which is given by Paul himself. It is the perverting and debasing effect of sin that darkens the mind and the understanding and makes fools of us, or, as the phrase, 'they became fools,' has been translated, 'they became silly.'

And if that was true of his day, it is equally true today. There is something rather pathetic in the way in which men during the past hundred years have fondly imagined that they have been doing something new and original in giving up the worshipping of God. The fact is that they have but repeated this old, old story, and the repetition has been perfect right down to the smallest detail. Nothing has been more characteristic of this whole tendency than the way in which men have given up religion always in terms of advance and enlightenment, knowledge and understanding, emancipation from bondage and tyranny, and liberty and freedom. It has almost become the hallmark of intelligence to scoff at religion.

That has been the claim. But what of the facts? Once more an exact repetition of the old story. And as was true in the story Paul had to unfold, so it is still true that this debasing influence of sin is as manifest and evident intellectually as well as morally, as much in theory as in practice. We can look at this along the following lines:

Consider the gods that men worship today and that they have worshipped especially during the past twenty years. The use of the terms 'gods' and 'worship' is perfectly justifiable. That is a man's god for which he lives, for which he is prepared to give his time, his energy, his money, that which stimulates him and rouses him, excites and enthuses him. He lives for it and is controlled by it, and is prepared to sacrifice all for it. What are the modern gods? First and foremost I would place 'man' himself. This may not have been quite as evident in the past two or three years, but prior to that the belief in man and his powers was almost endless. Nothing was impossible to man, and one of the strongest reasons for putting aside a belief in God was that that belief was an insult to man and imposed limits upon him. This belief in man has expressed itself in many different ways. Ultimately it is the explanation of Nazism and Bolshevism, the worship of race and blood and of the State. I am appalled at times at the number of people who worship England, and I suggest that much of the heroism that is being displayed today is often really the result of a definite worshipping of a code or a tradition. Other gods that are worshipped are money and wealth, the things that these can buy, such as houses and motor cars, social status and position. I have known parents who have literally worshipped their children. There was a time when it seemed clear that many were returning to a worshipping of the body and physical fitness, and one has but to glance at a newspaper to see that there has obviously been a marked and striking revival in the belief in astrology. I merely mention also the various cults that have flourished so much since the last war – theosophy, Christian Science and the popular psychological teaching which has told us to believe in ourselves, and to have faith in ourselves. I read a most interesting and provocative article which suggested that the ever-increasing number of pet animals kept by people was definitely a religious matter, and I need but mention the use of mascots. Such are the gods to whom men and women have turned, boasting as they have done so of their superiority over their fathers and forefathers, who worshipped the only true and living God. Comment is surely unnecessary.

Precisely the same thing is seen if we look at the way in which men spend their time, and contrast it with what was true when men believed in God and worshipped Him. Apart from the enormity of sin, I hate it and protest against it because of the way in which it insults man and debases all his powers and especially his highest powers. While men believed in God, they spent their time in a manner that was ennobling and uplifting. They were out to improve their minds. They read the best books they could find, and their conversation had reference to theology, politics, and other matters which called for the exercise of intelligence. And when I say this I am thinking not only of certain classes or of townspeople only. It was true in general, and of the country as well as the town. Is there anything which is more tragic than to compare and to contrast the average man of, say, fifty years ago and the corresponding man of today? The modern man lives on newspapers and periodicals, repeats the views of others without thinking for himself, and spends his time listening to the wireless or sitting in a cinema. In his talks and discussions he is interested chiefly in sport and gambling. Even his interest in politics had so degenerated, and he had become so apathetic, that he allowed himself to be governed for years by the dullest and most supine politicians that this country has ever known. Indeed, a good case can be made for saying that it was the slothfulness, and love of ease and pleasure, which characterized the majority of our people that accounted most directly for the present war. Crimes committed on the Continent which would have aroused the whole country fifty or sixty years ago were allowed to pass almost without a comment, leave alone a mighty protest. Intellectually as well as morally, we have been witnessing a sad decline, a decline that is the invariable consequent of worshipping and serving 'the creature more than the Creator, who is blessed for ever'.

(iii) But there is a further statement concerning sin made by St Paul. He says that it is also disgusting. And he is not content with merely making the statement. He illustrates it by giving us a picture of the kind of life that was lived at that time. He gives a list of the foul and ugly sins of which men and women were guilty and in which they gloated – the sexual perversions, 'fornication, wickedness, covetousness, maliciousness, full of envy, murder, debate, deceit, malignity, whisperers, backbiters, haters of God, despiteful, proud, boasters, inventors of evil things, disobedient to parents, without understanding, covenant-breakers, without natural affection, implacable, unmerciful' (Rom. 1:29-31) What a horrible list. How disgusting. The list itself can be easily subdivided. All I am concerned to do is to show the ugliness and foulness of it all, which is to be seen quite as much in covetousness, maliciousness, envy, deceit, malignity, whispering, backbiting, pride, etc., as it is in the grosser forms of sexual licence and perversion. The same lust and passion, the horrible 'burning' to which Paul refers, is found in all, though we have tended to pass some as being quite respectable! How futile and ridiculous it is to try to make light of sin when we think of the twists and contortions, the passion and the lust which are displayed in temper and malice, in jealousy and envy, and the way in which men and women plot and scheme to destroy each other socially and in other respects. There is but one word to describe it all – it is disgusting.

But again we must remind ourselves that this list of Paul's is as accurate a description of life today as it was then. What more perfect account is possible of our sex-ridden mentality, leading as it has done to promiscuity, infidelity, divorce and the moral muddle of present-day society? Life has become loud and ugly, decency and chastity are almost regarded as signs of weakness and incomplete development. Everything is justified in terms of self-expression, and the more animal we are the more perfect we are. The moral sense itself seems to be atrophied, for what Jeremiah said of his generation can be said of ours: 'Were they ashamed when they had committed abomination? Nay they were not at all ashamed neither could they blush' (Jer. 8:12). What an indictment! Beyond blushing – sunk and wallowing in the mire!

Such is the problem with which we are confronted. There is in us, in man, this terrible, mighty power called 'sin' which alienates us from God and leads us to hate Him, and at the same time debases us and leads us to conduct which can only be described as disgusting. How idle it is to think of these matters and to discuss them theoretically. How criminal to look at life through rose-coloured spectacles. It is only as we face the facts, and realize the true nature of the problem, that we shall come to see that one power alone is sufficient and adequate to deal with it – the power of God.

~ *Chapter Four* ~

The
Wrath
of
God

~ *Chapter Four* ~

The
Wrath of God

Romans 1:18

> 'For the wrath of God is revealed from heaven against all
> ungodliness and unrighteousness of men, who hold the
> truth in unrighteousness.'

In this verse the Apostle begins to show the need for the
gospel which he has just been extolling. He has been
describing its nature and showing the only way by which
it and its benefits can be received. He has also referred to
the sense of urgency which he himself felt in the work of
proclaiming the gospel. And now he begins to illustrate all
that in terms of the human situation. Why is the preaching
of the gospel such an urgent matter? The answer is 'that
the wrath of God is revealed from heaven against all

ungodliness and unrighteousness of men.' Why is salvation
entirely a matter of faith? The reply is that the whole
world, Jews and Gentiles alike, are hopelessly guilty before
God. Why will nothing that is less than the power of God
unto salvation meet the situation? The answer is the havoc
wrought by sin both on man's standing in the presence of
God and also upon man's nature.

But the Apostle starts with that which is most urgent
and most central of all – the wrath of God. He states it
as a fact and then proceeds to consider the cause of the
wrath and its manifestation. We, in the previous lectures,
have adopted the reverse order. We have stated the case
and examined the situation first, in order that we may
show how all this must of necessity call forth the wrath
of God. We have done so deliberately and for the reason
that we have repeated on each occasion – namely, that
the situation with which we are confronted has a new
element in it which makes that procedure a necessity. The
trouble in St Paul's day, as he tells us in verse 32, was
not that man denied or disbelieved in the wrath of God,
but rather that, though they knew the judgment of God
against sin and wrongdoing, they nevertheless continued
to sin and to take pleasure in others who did the same.
Now that was once the case in this country. But during
the past century it has certainly ceased to be the case.
Men no longer ignore the doctrine, or sin in spite of it;
they deny it, they dispute it, and indeed entirely reject
it. That is the situation with which we have to deal, and
with which we propose to engage ourselves now.

In a sense, we are still dealing with the question and the problem of sin. But we are concerned about it in its godward aspect rather than in terms of man as in the last lecture.

There is one aspect of this question of the wrath of God which we must note, in which it differs somewhat from the questions with which we have been engaged hitherto. In the main, but not entirely so, it has been true to say with regard to the fallacies concerning man's attitude towards morality, and his hopelessly inadequate view of sin, that they belong to the world outside the Church. But when we come to this particular question of the wrath of God, and the attitude of men towards it, we are considering the situation within the Church quite as much, if not indeed more so, as the situation which exists without. Personally, I would hazard the opinion that one of the main factors in the explanation of the loss of authority on the part of the Church recently, has been her increasing departure from this doctrine. At first, it was muffled, then for a while it was not mentioned at all, and, finally, it was openly attacked and denied.

It can be said with certainty that there is no doctrine which is so generally repugnant to the majority of men as this particular doctrine. We said that the doctrine of sin unfolded in the Bible was ridiculed by many, but amongst those who accept the teaching concerning sin there are many who entirely reject the teaching concerning the wrath of God.

To those outside the Church and whose view of man is the very antithesis of that seen in the Bible, this doctrine presents no real difficulty at all. It is something that can be dismissed very easily. Their theory about comparative religion and the development of man provides a ready explanation. This doctrine is nothing but a survival of the instinct of fear projected on to the belief in God. It is just a relic of the primitive state, a survival from the days of taboos when man was so ignorant that he had to be coerced into living the right kind of life. Indeed, some would explain the whole thing quite easily in terms of psychology. Langdon Brown, in his *Thus We are Men*, says quite definitely and dogmatically that the decline in the belief in the wrath of God has been parallel with the gradual disappearance of the stern, autocratic, harsh Victorian type of father! In other words, the idea is that men in the past projected on to God the complexes which had been created within them by their own fathers. We do not stop to show how utterly superficial that view is. The mere citing of innumerable cases of men who had over-indulgent fathers, but nevertheless believed in the wrath of God, would be more than sufficient in and of itself. This, quite apart from the further evidence provided by men whose fathers had been veritable tyrants, who yet rejected *in toto* belief in the wrath of God. We do not stop with that, because we are anxious to deal with this matter on a deeper level. For the real trouble with people in that position is that they do not really believe in God at all.

But apart from them there has been an increasing objection to the whole idea of the wrath of God, and that on the part of people who are deeply concerned about the question of religion. The cause of the objection at times has been the feeling that the idea of wrath is not consistent with the idea of love in God. It is not that they deny the idea altogether, but that they cannot reconcile it with the doctrine of God's love of which they are sure. Others go further and deny the idea of wrath altogether, and say that to speak of wrath in God is to misrepresent His character very seriously. To such people there appears to be but one attribute in God and that is His love. They never mention His other attributes, such as righteousness and holiness and justice. All ideas that are associated with such attributes are distasteful to them, such as equity and judgment and punishment. They so emphasize the love of God as to give the impression that the New Testament simply says that 'God is love,' forgetting that it also says that 'God is light and in Him is no darkness at all' (1 John 1:5). Others take up the position of saying that whatever may be the truth about this matter of the wrath of God, it is clearly unwise to preach it and to emphasize it. They call our attention to the great change that has taken place in the condition of mankind from the standpoint of intellect and knowledge. They grant that, formerly, preaching and teaching which emphasized that aspect of the truth may have been quite useful, but that, nowadays, men resent the very suggestion of threats and are likely to be antagonized from the gospel by such methods. On the other hand, we are told, men and women today, in their state of enlightenment, are always ready to hearken unto and respond to an appeal. They refuse to be coerced or driven, but are ever ready to respond to the call of love.

Whatever the form of the objection may have been, all who are familiar with the facts will be ready to agree that, during the past fifty years, very little has been heard about the wrath of God. The whole emphasis has been placed upon the love of God, almost to the exclusion of all else. The effects and repercussions of this have been very widespread – much more so than we often realize. Its effect in the world of theology has been profound, and especially with reference to the most central of all the doctrines, namely the doctrine of the death of Christ and the Atonement. The expiatory or piacular view of the death of Christ has become almost unknown; the idea of a mighty transaction by God in which sin was dealt with and punished in our Lord's body on the Cross, is scarcely known at all. The Cross has become nothing but a manifestation and demonstration of the love of God. We cannot stay with this, but we note it as a direct consequence of the rejection of the doctrine of the wrath of God. In precisely the same way, the doctrine of justification by faith only has passed into desuetude. Increasingly salvation has been represented as an action on the part of man, and God is depicted as just waiting patiently in an attitude of love for us to return. Apart from encouraging us to return, He is entirely passive. In other words, it is obvious that the rejection of the idea that there is such a thing as the wrath of God with respect to sin must affect the whole of Christian theology. And it has done so. But it has affected many other spheres of life also. It has greatly influenced the whole question of the home and the upbringing of children. In the same way it has entered deeply into the educational system. And again, the effects of this teaching are seen clearly in the matter of prison reform and the whole outlook upon the question of the punishment of crime and wrongdoing. The central idea has been, exactly as in the case of the gospel itself, to do away with the idea of reward and punishment, and to teach the importance of goodness for its own sake. Law and discipline, compulsion and an external standard of right and wrong, goodness and evil, have become increasingly unpopular. We are told that we must not regard God as a lawgiver who must deal with sin and punish it. We must not think of sin as leading to any punishment beyond that which we inflict upon ourselves as the result of sinning. And we must realize that the way to improve people is not to punish them when they have done wrong, but, rather, to manifest our love to them. We must have greater faith in man and in his essential goodness, and just encourage him to live a better life.

In other words, in religion and in secular matters, there has been this deep-rooted objection to the whole idea of a lawgiver and an external law with a system of rewards and punishments. The idea of authority has been regarded as being synonymous with tyranny. Man himself has become the standard, and nothing must be imposed upon him from the outside. There are even those who would say that the business of education is not so much to teach a child knowledge, as to draw out what is within the child. They would not force any child to learn the three Rs; the child itself is to decide what it is to be taught, according to its own likes and dislikes.

The whole idea of the wrath of God, therefore, is regarded as being based upon an entirely false view of God and also a false view of man. God as love cannot possibly punish or desire to punish. And man, if he is but handled properly and trained and taught in the right manner, will never need to be punished at all.

What have we to say to all this?

(i) We answer it first of all on the practical or pragmatic level. I mean by this that facts alone, and in and of themselves, serve to show that the arguments we have mentioned are false. Afterwards, we shall see that they are also false when judged by higher standards.

As we have indicated, much of the argument against belief in the doctrine of the wrath of God has been presented in a more or less utilitarian manner. The older type of preaching, we are told, would drive people away from our churches; whereas if we emphasized and stressed the love of God it would appeal to the people. The simple answer to that is that the facts indicate the exact opposite. It is as the idea of judgment and the wrath of God have fallen into the background that our churches have become increasingly empty. The idea has gained currency that the love of God somehow covers everything, and that it matters very little what we may do, because the love of God will put everything right at the end. The more the Church has accommodated her message to suit the palate of the people, the greater has been the decline in attendance at places of worship.

But still more ominous is the fact that at the same time belief in God has also declined. As men cease to believe in God as the Lord of all the earth, and as the Judge Eternal before whom we shall all appear to render an account of ourselves, and as the impression is given more and more that

God is just some benign being who smiles indiscriminately upon all, so men have ceased to believe in Him and to relate their lives to Him.

It is simply not true to say that if only we emphasize constantly the love of God men will believe in Him, whereas if we preach His wrath and justice and righteousness they will be antagonized from Him. It is only as men know something of the meaning of 'the fear of the Lord' that they continue to believe in God.

In exactly the same way, the argument that the modern man refuses to be coerced into living the good life by the fear of God, but will respond to appeals, is entirely falsified by the facts. We have seen this already in a previous lecture. I content myself with saying that as men have ceased to believe in the wrath of God, and have discarded the idea of law and righteousness, so their moral standards have gradually deteriorated and conduct has become lax and loose.

With regard to the argument that the belief in the wrath of God has vanished as a result of the disappearance of the Victorian type of stern father, the facts surely are these. As men ceased to recognize God as the One to whom they are responsible, and under whose eye they live, so a sense of discipline and order gradually began to disappear from all the relationships of life. A man who does not live a life of obedience himself soon ceases to be concerned about the fact that his own children should obey him. The result is that discipline in the home has been sadly neglected, children no longer respect their parents as they should, and quite frequently these children have become the tyrants of the home. The fact is that those who were brought up under the stern and strict, and often hard discipline of former times, had actually a deeper regard as well as a greater respect for their parents. The criticism that belief in the wrath of God has gone as a result of the disappearance of the Victorian type of parent is superficial, were it merely that it does not face the question as to why parents ceased to behave in that manner, what led them to do so? It cannot be attributed to increase of knowledge and learning, for many parents had had that in times past without changing in this respect. No explanation that can be suggested is adequate save the one we are offering. As man's sense of responsibility to God has declined, and as he has ceased to believe that God has ordained the whole of life, including the natural orders of society, so the ideas of the family and home, of marriage and parenthood, and, indeed, of law and order in general, have become looser and looser, and men have regarded themselves as being laws unto themselves. And what real hope can there be of international peace and concord unless the nations are prepared to recognize and acknowledge a law above themselves and outside themselves — a law which has sanctions and power, a law the breaking of which will lead to suffering and punishment?

The theory that we have outgrown the idea of the wrath of God, which may have been helpful and useful in the past, is utterly exploded by a mere consideration of the facts.

(ii) But perhaps we have tarried too long with the argument at that level. We have done so in order to show its hollowness and shallowness when judged in terms of ordinary observation of the facts of life. But we have something of infinitely greater importance to consider. 'The wrath of God is revealed from heaven.' It is not a matter of opinion or of argument; it is a fact. It has been revealed. It matters not at all what men may think or say or decide. In our cleverness, we make our own gods, or we take out of God everything that is hateful and repugnant to our natural minds, and fondly imagine that all is well. What a fool's paradise! How ridiculous and childish it all is, quite apart from its arrogance! It is not only pure theory which, as we have seen, cannot produce any facts to justify itself; it is a direct denial of what has been revealed concerning God. That men who do not believe in God at all reject the idea of wrath is something to be expected. What is astonishing is that anyone who believes at all in the category of revelation, and who accepts what is shown concerning the love of God, should reject what is shown equally clearly concerning the wrath of God. The wrath is as vital and as integral a part of the revelation as the love. Indeed, that is the very nerve of Paul's argument at this point. It is because the wrath of God against sin has already been revealed that he is so proud of the gospel which is the revelation of God's way of salvation.

But how is this wrath of God revealed? Let us be careful, as we consider this, to remember that God's wrath must not be thought of in the way in which we usually think of it as applied to men. It does not mean impatience or uncontrolled anger. There is nothing arbitrary or unjust about it. It represents, rather, God's hatred of sin and wrongdoing, the utter antagonism of His holiness to sin, and His righteous anger against this rebellious power that has entered into the world and life, and which has wrought such havoc among His creatures.

This wrath has been revealed. How? We can but review the answer to that question briefly.

There is, first, what we may call 'general revelation'.

It is surely revealed in the realm of Nature itself, where there is clearly a law which sees to it that any transgression is followed by pain and suffering. If we ignore certain laws, we have to bear the consequences of subsequent pain. This can be illustrated in the matter of health. If we neglect it, we shall suffer. If we deliberately do something to harm it or endanger it, we shall suffer. We are not free agents in the sense that we can do anything we like freely or carelessly. If we deny the Giver of the law, we most certainly cannot dispute the fact of the law.

But even before we come to actions and their consequences, there is the fact of conscience. We have a sense of right and wrong and we know that certain things should not be done. As Paul puts it in the fifteenth verse of the next chapter: 'Which show the work of the law written in their hearts, their conscience also bearing witness, and their thoughts the meanwhile accusing or else excusing one another' (Rom. 2:15). If we try to explain away our own conscience and to deny its validity, in our judgment of other people and our censures on their actions, we again rehabilitate it. For thereby we announce that there is a standard of judgment and that there is a sense or even a law of right and wrong and of justice. There is a universal feeling in mankind that wrong should be punished, and that evil actions should bear their own consequences.

But, turning to the Bible, the revelation is still stronger and more explicit. The wrath of God is part of the special revelation of the Bible. And it is to be found in both the Old Testament and the New.

It is clearly the explanation of the state of the world that is offered in Genesis. Labour and sorrow, and toil and sweat, are the punishment of sin, and the fact that Nature is 'red in tooth and claw' is attributed to the same source. Man is condemned to his present mode of life as the result of his sin against God.

Likewise, the real purpose behind the giving of the Law was to reveal the holiness of God, His hatred of sin, His determination to punish sin. The Law was not meant to provide a way of salvation; it was given, according to Paul, to show 'the exceeding sinfulness of sin,' (Rom. 7:13) to reveal what God thought of sin, and what God would do about sin in the case of all who refused to accept His grace. The Law 'shut us up to Christ'; it makes us see our desperate need of Him in the light of the condemnation of sin.

In precisely the same way, it is central in the message of the prophets. The prophets did not merely call for reform and indicate the new way in which the nation should walk. They did not stop at, and with, the call to repentance. Indeed, the very urgency with which they called for repentance was due to the fact that the 'Day of the Lord,' the day of judgment, the day of doom was at hand. 'Seek ye the Lord while He may be found,' cries Isaiah (Isa. 55:6); 'It may be ye shall be hid in the day of the Lord's anger,' says Zephaniah (Zeph. 2:3). With Malachi, they all saw the coming of 'the day that shall burn as an oven' (Mal. 4:1). The prophets were not merely ethical teachers; they were sent primarily to call upon Israel to save herself from the Nemesis to which her sin was inevitably leading.

But right through the history of the children of Israel in the Old Testament this teaching concerning the wrath of God is constantly being revealed. All the troubles and tragedies of individuals and of the nations as a whole are explained in this way. Their forgetfulness of God and their departure from Him always leads to trouble. God punishes their transgressions, sometimes actively, sometimes passively, by allowing them to follow their own course and to reap the consequences of such a policy. The captivity in Babylon was not the result of political failure and military defeat primarily. It was the direct result of forsaking God; it was the wrath of God revealing itself against their sin. And in exactly the same way the events of A.D. 70, the sacking of Jerusalem and the hurling of the Jewish nation from their country, and the destruction of their temple, are but the literal fulfilling of what they had been told repeatedly would happen if they failed to repent. The story of the Chosen People is surely a terrifying object lesson of the doctrine of the wrath of God against sin.

We need but mention the name of John the Baptist to remind ourselves of the words, 'flee from the wrath to come' (Luke 3:7). As the last of the prophets, he epitomizes the prophetic message in that burning phrase.

Of the Coming One he says: 'whose fan is in His hand and He shall thoroughly purge His floor and will gather His wheat into the garner, but the chaff He will burn with the unquenchable fire' (Matt. 3:12).

But the teaching is equally clear and definite in our Lord's own ministry. We can but note a few instances. Think of it in Matthew 7: 'every tree that bringeth not forth good fruit is hewn down and cast into the fire' (v. 19). Again: 'depart from Me ye that work iniquity' (v. 23). Or think of the words He uses when addressing the disciples on the question of the fear of men: 'Fear not them which kill the body ... but are not able to destroy both soul and body in hell' (Matt. 10:28). And again think of the pictures of the judgment in Matthew 25 and in Luke 13: 23-30, and in His references to the City of Jerusalem. Also John 3:36: 'the wrath of God abideth on him.'

The same is seen clearly in the teaching of the Acts, with its clarion call, 'save yourselves from this untoward generation,' (Acts 2:40) and everywhere in the teaching of the Epistles. But we must note particularly the exposition of the revelation of the wrath of God given by St Paul in verses 24, 26 and 28 of his first chapter of the Epistle to the Romans. According to Paul, God punished the sin of those who had rejected Him and turned away from Him, and who had made their own gods – God punished the sin of the ancient pagan world and revealed His wrath against it in the following way: He 'gave them up to uncleanness through the lusts of their own hearts, to dishonour their own bodies between themselves' (v. 24). 'He gave them over to a reprobate mind to do those things which are not convenient' (v. 28). In other words, the actual state of the ancient pagan world is a demonstration of the wrath of God. God punished sin by ceasing to restrain it, by allowing it to take its own course and to work itself out. He gave over the people to a reprobate mind. The more they denied Him and ignored Him, the more, in a sense, were they proclaiming His being. We tend to think that the wrath of God must manifest itself in the form of active punishment, but here we are reminded that sometimes it reveals itself by just allowing sin to run riot, and, in an utterly unrestrained way, to show itself in all its foulness, ugliness and horror. Surely this is of tremendous significance at the present time. Is not this the explanation of the present state of the world and of mankind? We have set up our own ideas of God and our philosophies in the place of revelation, we have tried to construct a new Jesus, and we have ordered and lived our lives according to our ideas, not God's. For a century this apostasy has been proceeding, and men have boasted of the new world they were going to make. For a while all seemed well. Nothing terrible happened, and towards the end of the last century, and the early years of the present century, the perfect era seemed to have arrived. But since then we have had the two most terrible wars of history, and life has deteriorated and degenerated in the way we have already seen. What does it all mean? It is but a repetition of what Paul says: 'God has given us over to a reprobate mind.' We have been allowed to reap that which we have sown. It is God's judgment upon us, not in the sense that He has caused or sent war, but that He has allowed our sin to work itself out and to lead to its inevitable consequences of suffering and pain. The state of the world at the present hour proclaims loudly 'the wrath of God against all ungodliness and sin'. If we deny this truth, therefore, it just means that we claim to know more about God than did the prophets, the apostles, and even Christ Himself.

I hesitate to add anything further. I am not at all sure but that the supreme need of the present hour is preaching that will proclaim and announce 'the wrath of God against all ungodliness and sin' without any argument or appeal. The lessons of the present state of the world should be enforced, and we should warn the people that, unless they repent, worse may yet come to pass. Whatever we may think or say, as we have seen, the fact of God's wrath against sin is plainly and clearly revealed in so many different ways. And yet I would add a few words by way of answer to objections.

There is nothing so arrogant, or so dangerous, as to use the type of argument which says that we should not believe anything concerning God which we cannot believe of man. This argument sounds very plausible, but it conceals two fundamental fallacies. The first is the failure to understand the meaning of the word 'wrath', and to think of it in terms of sinful human wrath. The second is the failure to realize the holiness of God and His essential difference from us. 'God is light and in Him is no darkness at all' (1 John 1:5). We can scarcely conceive of that, and for that reason any attempt on our part to postulate what may or may not be true of God is mere ignorant guesswork. God's justice and righteousness and holiness demand and insist upon His hatred of sin and all its works. Anything else is inconceivable.

But this does not imply for a moment, as so many seem to think, that God is therefore not a God of love. Indeed, it does the exact opposite. It is only in the light of God's hatred and abhorrence of sin that we can really see His love, and appreciate the wonder and the glory of the gospel. The measure of His anger against sin is the measure of the love that is prepared to forgive the sinner and to love him in spite of the sin. In spite of all the talk and writing about the love of God during the past century, there has been much less evidence of true appreciation of the love of God and less readiness to surrender all to it. The idea of love has been so sentimentalized that it has become little more or better than a vague general benevolence. The love of God is a holy love. It expresses itself not by condoning sin or compromising with it; it deals with it, and yet does so in such a way that the sinner is not destroyed with his sin, but is delivered from it and its consequences. As our Lord points out in the parable He spoke to Simon the Pharisee (Luke 7), it is only as we realize our sinfulness in the sight of God that we can truly appreciate His love – 'to whom much is forgiven the same loveth much' (v. 47).

But, finally, there is no real ground at all for the objection to this teaching concerning 'the wrath of God'. For the way of escape is wide open. There is no need for anyone to remain under the wrath of God. And surely that fact settles the matter. Were there no escape, the position would be very different. But what can happen to anyone who deliberately refuses to accept that offer of salvation save to suffer the consequences of that refusal? And that is the explanation of the note of urgency in the preaching of

Paul and the other apostles, and of all the greatest preachers ever since. That is why the gospel is good news. The wrath of God is already revealed. But now the way to escape that wrath is also revealed in the gospel of Christ. To argue about, and to object to the wrath, and in the meantime to ignore the announcement concerning the love and the grace, is not only the height of folly, it is also to condemn oneself to needless suffering and punishment; and at the same time it robs us of every excuse and plea.

~ Chapter Five ~
The
Only
Solution

~ Chapter Five ~
The Only Solution

Romans 1:16

> 'For I am not ashamed of the gospel of Christ: for it is the power of God unto salvation to every one that believeth; to the Jew first, and also to the Greek.'

In these words, St Paul introduces the fundamental theme of this great Epistle. All that follows is but the working out of this proposition. The word 'for' at the beginning connects it with what he had just been saying. He has a message, something to give to the Greeks and to the Barbarians, to the wise and to the unwise. And in the same way, he adds, he is prepared to preach the gospel in Rome also. Indeed, he is longing to do so and has several times purposed to do so. For he is 'not ashamed of the gospel of Christ' which he preaches.

Now we must be perfectly clear in our minds as to the nature of the expression which he uses. It is what is called a litotes – the use of a negative to express a positive. It is a form of speech which is said to characterize the Englishman who is afraid to claim too much, and who, when he intends to say that we are doing really well in any department of the war, expresses it by saying that 'we have no reason to be dissatisfied with the progress hitherto made'. In other words, the Apostle means that he is proud of the gospel and glories in it.

But why did he use the negative form? Even a cursory reading of his Epistles shows clearly that it is not to be explained solely as a matter of temperament in this case. It actually adds to the strength of the statement. This we can see clearly if we but recall to our minds some of the facts concerning the great city of Rome, in which the people to whom the Apostle wrote these words lived. What was true of Rome was true also, of course, of other cities in which Paul had preached, such as Athens and Corinth. But Rome was after all the great metropolis of the world at that time. She was the seat of the Imperial Government, which governed the whole of the world that counted then, and she, therefore, attracted unto herself everything that was prized and valued most of all. Thus all the representatives of the various religions and schools of philosophy and of thought made their way there. But, above all else, Rome was famous for her law and her system of government. She was thus a proud city – the proudest city of the world. She boasted of her wealth and power, her learning and her culture, her religions and her polity; and her great buildings were famous everywhere. She seemed to be the perfect city, and in her human culture and progress seemed to have reached her very zenith. She was indeed the very embodiment of pride in human greatness and achievement, in a sense that scarcely any other city has ever been since then. This spirit she showed in particular in her attitude to the Christian religion. Many official and unofficial records bear testimony to this. To her nothing could be so ludicrous as the claim of the gospel. To suggest that a small, insignificant sect of people, who belonged mainly to one of the poorest of their colonies and conquered territories, should possess the message that the whole of mankind needed was ridiculous. And the utter folly of such an idea was further demonstrated when it became clear that the very essence of that message was to believe that a man who belonged to one of the most despised towns, even of that country, and who, far from being a great scholar or philosopher, was just a common carpenter, was the unique Son of God. But what finally made such a claim sheer madness was the fact that He, far from being a great powerful conqueror who had subdued nations to Himself by His might and power, was actually crucified in utter weakness and helplessness between two thieves. This entire claim of the despised sect called Christian was folly to the Greeks, with their ideas of philosophy; to the Romans it was even worse. Its sheer weakness was an offence, apart from anything else.

Now, it was to people who lived in an atmosphere of that kind that Paul utters these words. To the proud, cultured, self-satisfied metropolis of the world, with all

its wealth and power, he is prepared to preach his gospel
– nay, he longs to do so. He knows what Rome thinks
of it and that she regards all who believe and preach it
as being beneath contempt. But that does not worry him
nor affect him. And when he gets there he will not feel
crestfallen, or deem it necessary to apologise for himself
or his message. For he is proud of it, he glories in it,
he boasts of it and exults in it. To him it is something
compared with which all that Rome is, and can boast of,
pales into insignificance. Rome would try to pour ridicule,
contempt, and shame upon any who believed it. She had
done so and would continue to do so. But, knowing all
about her and her proud claim, Paul is not ashamed, for
he knows that what he preaches is needed by Rome as
by every other place, and that it infinitely transcends in
worth all they have and all they believe.

Now, it must be quite clear to all that the situation
which confronts the gospel and its preaching at the present
time, in this and most other countries, is strangely similar
to that which we have been describing. There was a time
when it was true to say of the masses of the people that
their position was one in which they recognized the truth
of the gospel, and admitted and acknowledged that it was
right, but failed to put it into practice. They may have gone
further and have objected to its stringent ethical and moral
demands. But even then they were paying tribute to it, and
merely putting up defences for their own sin and weaknesses.
The gospel in those days was recognized as presenting the
highest and the best way of life. Indeed, according to some,
it was such a high and noble way as to be impossible and

impracticable. They therefore paid it lip service, but failed to practise it. That was once the position. But it is no longer so. A great change has taken place, and we are back in a position such as obtained in Rome in the time of St Paul. The general attitude towards the gospel has changed completely. From being recognized as right and true, it went through a phase when it was patronized and ignored. But by today it is being actively attacked and opposed. Indeed, we have even reached a stage beyond that: it is being ridiculed and dismissed. The claim today is that it is something which no educated, reasonable person can possibly accept and believe. It is placed in the category of folklore and superstition, and regarded as a mere survival of the days when men, in their ignorance, were the slaves of various fears and phobias. All this can be proved, it is contended, by the advance of knowledge, the result of scientific discovery, and the light which psychology has thrown on human nature and its strange behaviour. Certain aspects of the moral teaching of the gospel are accepted and praised, though some would even reject that, but as for the central claims of the gospel – namely, the unique deity of Christ, the miracles He worked while on earth, His atoning death and literal physical resurrection, the Person of the Holy Spirit and the claims of the early chapters of the Book of Acts – all these things are rejected with contempt and sarcasm. It has become the hallmark of culture and learning to be irreligious or anti-religious. Nay, further, to believe in the gospel is regarded as one of the greatest hindrances to true progress and development. Salvation is to be found, according to the modern man, in the full use of the human capacities and powers which can be trained by knowledge and education. Man must save himself, man can save himself. He has it within him to do so. That is the essence of the modern creed. And if anyone ventures to mention the gospel of Christ, with its offer of a miraculous salvation, he is regarded as being so hopelessly behind the times as to be almost an idiot. Furthermore, should he press this message, he is regarded as being insulting, and as doing something which might have been legitimate hundreds of years ago when man was ignorant and primitive, or which might still be all right in the case of the unenlightened savages in the wilds of Africa. And were he to go further and say that the gospel is the only hope for mankind, individually and collectively, he would be roared at as a lunatic or a fool.

Nevertheless, that is precisely and exactly what we assert today, as Paul did so long ago. And we do so without any sense of shame or apology. Furthermore, our reasons for doing so are precisely those that animated Paul, the reasons which have led all others to do the same through the passing ages and centuries.

With such a glowing and glorious text, we shall confine ourselves mainly to a positive statement, referring only in passing, by way of criticism, to the pathetic and foolish talk and claims of those who reject it. Indeed, there is little need to spend time in negative criticism. We need but point to the state of the world today, which is nothing but an appalling monument to human failure. We might add a request that those who reject the gospel, in a manner which is so reminiscent of the attitude of ancient Rome, should acquaint themselves with the subsequent history of that proud, cultured and powerful city, and of other cities and countries that have maintained a similar attitude.

No! We do not hesitate to state that the only hope for men is to believe the gospel of Christ. We say so knowing full well all the talk about science and learning and culture. We say so knowing that, at the end of this war, the world, in exactly the same way as at the end of the last war, will announce with confidence its plans and schemes for a new world, without taking any account of what the gospel has to say. Why do we say so? For precisely the same reasons adduced by St Paul in the words of our text. He states them quite clearly:

(i) First and foremost, he is proud of the gospel because it is God's way of salvation. Herein it differs from all else that has ever been offered to mankind as a view of life and a way of life; and therein lies always the main and chief reason why we should boast of it and exult in it. But let us analyse this a little and see more fully what it implies.

At once we see that it possesses an authority which is quite unique. For all other ideas with respect to life and its problems are man-made. At their best and highest, they never get beyond the realm of speculation and supposition. Sometimes they speak with an arrogant dogmatism and certainty, ever a characteristic of the lesser minds. The great minds and the profoundest thinkers have always acknowledged and confessed that they do not know. They have always been content to describe themselves as seekers.

Their language always is 'I think,' 'I opine,' 'I imagine,' 'I suppose,' 'It surely must be the case.' They do not know, and they end by admitting that the ultimate problems of life are shrouded in mystery which is impenetrable to the human mind and its powers. The very fact that there are so many different and differing schools of thought bears eloquent testimony to this uncertainty and inability. The ancient world in which Paul lived had witnessed the rise of many schools of philosophy, each having its proponents and champions, and each claiming to approximate more closely to the ultimate truth and reality than any other. Some made their boast in Aristotle, others in Plato, others in Socrates, others in Zeno. But all the systems ultimately ended on a query. Each displayed great learning and much understanding, and each had its system. But there was another fact in the ancient world that proved how inadequate all the schools were finally. And that was the endless number of religions that were to be found. Thought alone was known to be insufficient. There was something behind the world; there were unseen powers and agencies. Life could not be explained without invoking the gods. And the Roman Empire was full of the various religions devoted to the worshipping of these gods and their corresponding temples. We see a perfect picture of this in Acts 17 as regards Athens. The same was true of Rome and all other great cities. With all their pomp and show and their pride and learning, they had nothing but uncertainty and the spirit of fear. They boasted of the names of their great men and their great philosophic systems. But how empty was their boasting. The great men themselves had to acknowledge that they did not know, and suicide was increasingly common even among them. How foolish to boast of a man's brainpower and understanding and insight, and the wonderful nature of his thought processes, if finally they lead nowhere. But Paul had something essentially different to offer and to preach. He knew of the other systems. But he also knew their limits and their inability to solve the problems. He could not make his boast in men and their systems. Before he could boast of a system it must have authority; it must have certainty.

It must not be a mere approximation to the truth, but the Truth itself. Speculations could not save, but the gospel Paul preached was not speculation; it was a revelation from God Himself. As he says in writing to the Galatians: 'But I certify you, brethren, that the gospel which was preached of me is not after man. For I neither received it of man, neither was I taught it, but by the revelation of Jesus Christ' (Gal. 1:11-12). There was no need to be ashamed of such a message. And it is precisely the same today. Take all the writing, preaching and teaching of the past hundred years. In a sense, human ability and effort have never exerted themselves to such an extent. Philosophy has been glorified and man has claimed that he could solve the riddle of life and of the universe. Never has man been so proud of himself and his achievements and his understanding. But what has been the result of all this? What of life today? Is it not clear that we are precisely in the same position as was the world in the time of Paul? Oh, the tragedy of it all! We have boasted of processes and systems, but they have yielded no results. We have taken pride in our ability to think, but it is the function of thinking to arrive at valid conclusions. Let us be honest. Are we any nearer to the solution of the problems of life and living than the philosophers were who lived and died before Paul? The answer is to be found in the state of the modern world. Our knowledge has grown merely with respect to the externals of life, its amenities and pleasures. Life itself still remains an enigma, and the art of living seems to be as elusive as ever. The rival systems still fail and cannot satisfy our needs. But the gospel is not a human philosophy. It is not man's idea or the result of man's effort and seeking. It is the revelation of what God thinks and says concerning life.

But let us be careful to observe also, that the gospel is not merely a statement of what God desires and expects of us. It is no mere ethical and moral programme or social scheme. It is not simply a call to a higher and nobler kind of life. That was true, in a sense, of the Old Testament and its revelation, but mankind had completely failed to respond to it. The gospel of Christ is not a repetition of that in a still more impossible form. It is not, then, solely the revelation of what God expects of us, and the pattern of life to which He would have us conform. It is that, but according to Paul it is something still more wonderful. Were it merely that, it would be something to boast of and to glory in, for it is a mode of life which is infinitely higher than anything ever produced by man. But, finally, we could not exult and glory in it, for it would simply spell our damnation and proclaim our final failure and doom.

No, the glory of the gospel is that it is primarily an announcement of what God does, and has done, in the

Person of Jesus Christ. That was the essence of Paul's gospel, as he proceeds to show in the remainder of the Epistle. That was the gospel which was preached by all the apostles. They preached Jesus as the Christ. They made a proclamation, an announcement. Primarily, they called upon people to listen to what they called 'good news'. They did not in the first instance outline a programme for life and living. They were not setters forth of a point of view which they called upon people to accept. They did not go round the world in the first instance propagating a new order or a new scheme for living. They began by stating facts and explaining what they meant. They preached, not a programme, but a Person. They said that Jesus of Nazareth was the Son of God come from Heaven to earth. They said that He manifested and demonstrated His unique deity by living a perfect, spotless, sinless life of complete obedience to God, and by performing miracles. His death on the Cross was not merely the end of His life as the result of His rejection by His own countrymen; it had a deeper and more eternal significance. It was something that had to happen in order that mankind might be reconciled to God. It was a transaction between God the Father and God the Son. It was the Son bearing our sins 'in His own body on the tree', and the fulfilment of the ancient prophecy of Isaiah, who had said that the Messiah would be 'wounded for our transgressions,' and that 'with his stripes we shall be healed' (Isa. 53:5). Indeed, as Paul put it elsewhere, 'God was in Christ reconciling the world unto himself' (2 Cor. 5:19). But that was not all. He had risen from the grave, had manifested Himself unto certain chosen witnesses, and then ascended into Heaven. From Heaven He had sent the gift of the Holy Spirit upon the early Church, and He had brought unto them not only new understanding, but new life and power. Their lives had been entirely changed, and they now had life which was life indeed. That was the message. Its entire emphasis was upon what God had done. Its content was God's way of salvation and of making men righteous. Man had but to accept it and submit to it. Here indeed was something to be proud of as a message. Here was something which enabled one to face Stoics and Epicureans at Athens without a blush or an apology; here was a message which made the world's highest and greatest philosophies appear to be nothing but the prattling and babbling of babes.

(ii) But a second reason for glorying in it and boasting of it *is that it works* — it is '*the power* of God unto salvation'. It is not surprising that Paul uses the word 'power' in writing to Rome. That was their great word. And they tended to judge everything in terms of power. Rome was the great Imperial City, and power was to Rome what wisdom was to Athens. They would not consider anything unless it worked and had power. It mattered little how noble and excellent a thing might be in itself, how sublime as a conception, unless it worked and produced the results. The Romans were essentially pragmatic and utilitarian in their outlook. That was their test and standard. Paul knew that, and it was because he knew it that he uttered his challenge. Did they test a gospel by its results? Very well, he is ready to meet them. Nay, more; he is ready to challenge them. What had all their learning and culture and their multitude of religions really produced? If they were really interested in results – well, let them produce them. What was the type of life lived by the citizens of the Roman Empire? What was the level of their morality? And he proceeds to answer his own question in the words found from verse 18 to the end of the chapter. That was the kind of life the people lived. Is that success? Is that civilization and culture? Is that something of which to boast? What is the point and the value of all the philosophies if they cannot deal with the problems of life? They appear to be intellectual and are extremely interesting, but the business of a philosophy is not to raise problems, but to solve them. He, Paul himself, had once boasted of the Jewish Law and of his success in keeping it. But he came to see that all of which he had boasted was merely something external; when he came to see the real inner spiritual meaning of the law, he discovered that he was an utter failure. He works out that theme in chapter 15 of this letter. All man's efforts to solve the problems of life fail, whether they be along purely intellectual lines, or consist in moral effort and striving, or in painful trudging along the mystic way. But the gospel which he, Paul, now preached, works! It had worked in his own life. It had changed and transformed everything. It had brought peace and rest to his soul and given victory in his life. And it had done the same to countless thousands of others. How did it do so? Paul again answers the question in the immediate context.

The key to the answer is found in the fact that the gospel alone faces and exposes, and really deals with, the funda-mental problem of man and his needs. The gospel alone faces the facts in all their utter nakedness and horror; it alone has the right view of man as he is. Without a true anthropology, it is idle to discuss soteriology – diagnosis must precede treatment. The gospel is unique in both respects. It alone diagnoses accurately; it alone has the remedy. Let us observe its method of doing so. What are the main and chief problems of life and of man? Wherein are to be found the causes of our misery and failure, of life as it is today in this world? We have been considering them already in our previous discussions of this section.

First and foremost we are face to face with the fact of the wrath of God. Paul starts with that, because, obviously, it is the most important and serious matter of all. But, alas! It is the one thing of which mankind never thinks, the one thing which it never considers in all its calculations. All scheming and planning and thinking are purely in terms of man. And this is why they always fail and are always doomed to failure. How can you plan for life and the world and at the same time exclude God who is the Maker and Sustainer and Controller of all things? God has not only made the world, He is actively concerned in it, and constantly intervenes in its affairs. His laws are absolute and cannot be avoided. He has decreed that disobedience and evil and sin are to be punished, and one of the forms of punishment is to allow our actions to bear their own fruits and consequences, here and now, in this present world. God has decided and ordered and arranged that a life of forgetfulness of Him, and of antagonism to Him, shall not be successful and happy. Cursing falls upon such a way of life. That is the whole story of mankind from the very beginning, and it has continued until this day, and it will continue to be so until the end of time. Mankind has refused to recognize this – indeed, has ridiculed it. It has been confident that it could succeed without God. But what of the results? Constant failure. God cannot be thwarted. The facts of life, the story of history, proclaim the wrath of God against all ungodliness and unrighteousness. That is our first problem. We have sinned against God. We are in the wrong relationship to Him. His wrath is upon us. We have made it impossible for Him to bless us. His Holy nature demands that He must punish us and our transgressions. What can we do about it? Nothing! Our tears, our sorrow, our works and strivings, can avail nothing. We cannot atone for our past or undo our misdeeds, or make recompense. None can keep the law. 'There is none righteous, no, not one' (Rom. 3:10). 'Every mouth may be stopped.' The whole world is guilty before God (Rom. 3:19). Is there no hope, therefore? Can nothing be done? God be thanked, the gospel of Christ provides the answer, as we have already seen. God has dealt with our sins in Christ. The demands of holiness and justice have been satisfied—Christ has been 'delivered for our offences, and was raised again for our justification' (Rom. 4:25). God in Christ is prepared to receive us. In Him, who has 'been made a curse for us' (Gal. 3:13), the curse pronounced against sin is removed and there is hope for all. The law of God, which decrees travail and sorrow and misery as the result of sin, has been satisfied. God in Christ offers us pardon and forgiveness, and instead of cursing, blessing. Without God we cannot be happy, 'for there is no peace, saith my God, to the wicked.' Try as we will, and as mankind has, we cannot succeed. The first step is to have the favour of God, and in Christ it is gloriously possible – indeed, it is offered us.

But that raises another question. Why is it that man is in the wrong relationship? Why is it that man ever chooses to sin? The answer is that man has fallen away from God, and as a result, his whole nature has become perverted and sinful. Man's whole bias is away from God. By nature he hates God and feels that God is opposed to him. His god is himself, his own abilities and powers, his own desires. He objects to the whole idea of God and the demands which God makes upon him. We have seen this worked out in detail already in previous studies. Furthermore, man likes and covets the things that God prohibits, and dislikes the things and the kind of life to which God calls him. These are no mere dogmatic statements. They are facts. They alone explain the readiness of people to accept any theory, however flimsy and unsupported by facts and proofs, which queries and questions the being of God or the supernatural element in religion. They alone explain the moral muddle and the ugliness that characterize life to such an extent today. This is recognized, as regards the facts, by all serious thinkers. But all who are not Christian face the facts in such a superficial manner that their proposals with respect to them must of necessity fail. They are interested only in men's actions, and try to invent methods to persuade men to refrain from them. They write books and deliver lectures on the evil consequences of sin, both in the individual and socially; they paint their glowing pictures of the other type of life. But all this ignores the central problem, which is: Why should man ever desire the wrong? That is the question. Why is it that man, faced with good and evil, right and wrong, and knowing the consequences, the painful consequences, that follow wrongdoing, nevertheless chooses the wrong? And not merely ordinary or ignorant men, but all men, those who are most intellectual and cultured, those who spend their lives in considering these problems. Why is it? What explains it? Only one answer is satisfactory: that which is supplied by the gospel of Christ. Man's very nature is fallen. Man is wrong at the centre of his being, and therefore everything is wrong. He cannot be improved, for, finally, nothing will suffice but a radical change, a new nature. Man loves the darkness and hates the light. What can be done for him? Can he change himself? Can he renew his nature? 'Can the Ethiopian change his skin or the leopard his spots?' Can man change the whole bias of his life? Give him new clothing, provide him with a new house in new surroundings, entertain him with all that is best and most elevating, educate him and train his mind, enrich his soul with frequent doses of the finest culture ever known, do all this and more, but still he will remain the same essential man, and his desires and innermost life will be unchanged. Were that not true, the world and individual man would long since have reached perfection. Think of all the work of the philosophers and thinkers. Consider especially the titanic changes and social enactments of the past hundred years, with all the efforts at solving the problems of mankind. All these things are good and right in their way within their circumscribed limits. But the great problem is still left. Man needs a new nature. Whence can he obtain it? Again, there is but one answer, in Jesus Christ the Son of God. He came from Heaven and took upon Him human nature perfect and whole. He is God and man. In Him alone are the divine and the human united. And He offers to give us His own nature. He desires to make of us new men. He is 'the firstborn among many brethren' (Rom. 8:29). All who believe on Him, and receive Him, obtain this new nature, and as the result all things become different. Those who hated God now love Him and desire to know more and more about Him. Their supreme desire now is to please Him and to honour and to glorify Him. The things which formerly delighted them they now hate and detest, and the ways of God are the ways they desire. The self they glorified and which they ever desired to please, they now hate and regard as their greatest enemy. And this in turn brings them into an entirely new relationship with their fellow men. Loving the Lord their God first, they find themselves loving their neighbours as themselves. Self, and concern about self, is the great cause of all quarrelling and strife and war. Pride is the root of all social discord. But in Christ self is crucified and peace becomes truly possible. A new society is only possible when we have new men; and Christ alone can produce new men.

But, still, having said that, we are left with another great problem. Sin is not only something within us, it is a mighty power and force outside us. It entered human life from the outside and it attacked even the Son of God. That I am forgiven is glorious, that I have a new nature is wonderful and still better. But still I am left to face this terrible power that is set over against me, and which strives ever to defeat me, and to bring me into thraldom. It has defeated the mightiest and the strongest. It has not hesitated to match its strength even with God Himself. Its subtlety and its suggestions meet me everywhere. Who am I to confront such a foe? What is man at his best against such an antagonist? Who can conquer this Goliath that ever threatens us with defeat and ruin? Who can deliver us from this embodiment of the Philistines? Who can conquer this enemy that defeated Adam in all his perfection and innocence, and lured him to disgrace and death? Man cannot, for all men have failed. 'There is none righteous, no, not one' (Rom. 3:10). 'The whole world lieth in the evil one.' Satan has become 'the god of this world.' 'He is the strong man armed that keepeth his goods in peace.' Is all hopeless? Must we continue to strive and strive in vain? No! A David has appeared and smitten this Goliath; a Jonathan has routed the Philistines again. The Man has entered the lists and delivered the enemy a mortal wound from which he can never recover.

> 'O loving wisdom of our God!
> When all was sin and shame,
> A second Adam to the fight
> And to the rescue came.
>
> O wisest love! That flesh and blood,
> Which did in Adam fail,
> Should strive afresh against the foe,
> Should strive and should prevail.'

Jesus of Nazareth, the Son of God, has conquered Satan. Tried and tested to the utmost, He not only emerged unscathed, but hath 'cast out the prince of this world.' He has 'spoiled principalities and powers, making a show of them openly, triumphing over them in His Cross.' The Seed of the woman hath bruised the Serpent's head.(Gen. 3:15). He has conquered death and the grave and every power that is inimical to man and his highest interests. The Lion of the tribe of Judah has prevailed – yea, and not only for Himself, but for us. He offers us His own power and promises to clothe us with His own might. Not only need we not be defeated any longer; in Him we can become more than conquerors over any and every power that may raise itself against us.

These are the problems of the world, the problems of mankind, your problems and mine. They are exposed in the gospel and they are solved by it. Christ satisfies every need and He alone does so. He has 'done all things well'. The message of the gospel is about Him and what He has done. It is not theory. It works, it is a fact as the lives of Christians of all ages testify. Ashamed of it? A thousand times no! Ashamed rather of all else, our foolish pride, our empty pomp and show, our futile schemes and vain strivings that come to nought. No! No! 'I am not ashamed of the gospel of Christ, for it is the power of God unto salvation to every one that believeth.'

(iii) But the word 'everyone' leads us to the third great reason which Paul had for glorying in the gospel. It is God's way of salvation, it works, and, above all, it works for everyone, for anyone, for all. Here again is something in which it is quite unique. It is for the Jew first, but also for the Greek. It is for the wise and also for the unwise. No type or kind of person is excluded from its all-embracing scope and span. Here then is something in which one is truly entitled to boast. All the things about which others boasted, and in which they gloried, were sectional and partisan in their appeal and limited in the number of their adherents. They all lacked universality. Some religions made their appeal to a certain type of person; others to a different type. Philosophy only appealed to the wise and learned, and had nothing to give to the babes and sucklings and to the poor. There was not even one philosophy which appealed to all. There were the rival schools, and what satisfied one was rejected by another. Military might and power appealed to the strong and noble, and the ideals of law and justice had their own votaries. Nationalism appealed only to the citizens of the various countries, as Rome well knew in her attempts to subdue all to her own hegemony. The world was divided and discord prevailed. What one gloried in was anathema to another, and every attempt to produce something universal which would satisfy all had failed. How could one honestly boast therefore of any one of the various proposals?

But the gospel of Christ is entirely different. It is for anyone, for everyone. Its secret is that it postulates nothing in man except failure and sin and weakness. All those other ideas appeal only to certain types of psychological make-up and temperament, they have to presuppose something in us. And without that they fail of necessity.

A man glories in his own country and not in another; a man without brains and natural ability cannot truly learn and understand. And so on through the entire list of proposals and panaceas. But the gospel is not concerned about our natural differences. It centres on that which we share in common – sin and rebellion against God, failure in our lives, and a sense of shame. It demolishes all distinctions by placing us all together before God. And it does so, further, by postulating our weakness and helplessness, and relying for its efficacy upon the power of God Himself.

It matters not therefore who we are nor what we are. None can be too high or too low for this. There is no such thing as wise and unwise, great and small, learned and ignorant, wealthy or poor. There is no longer Jew and Gentile, Barbarian or Scythian, male or female, bond or free. God sees us as souls lost and desperate, helpless and forlorn. And He offers us the same salvation.

Others had been to Rome before Paul, great philosophers and teachers. They looked forward to addressing some – the great and the noble – but they had nothing to give to the poor. Paul is ready to preach to all – the Emperor on his throne, the counsellors and captains, but also the soldiers and the slaves, the outcast and despised. He has a message for all, and it is the same message for all. Ashamed of it? Why, it is the one thing which is worthy of our boasting and our exultation, for it alone is big enough and wide enough to deal with the whole world, and to include the praise of all.

How small and petty do the various things seem in which men make their boast, by the side of Jesus Christ and His gospel. Their appeal is but sectional, they lack power, and lead ever to nothing but failure and disappointment.

There is but one message that can include the whole world, in spite of all divisions and distinctions. There is but one power that can bring all men together and unite them and bring them to true brotherhood. There is but one solution to the problem of individual man and of the whole world. It is 'the gospel of Christ which is the power of God unto salvation to every one that believeth.'

All who have ever believed it, and have proved its truth and power, have joined Paul in saying and singing: 'God forbid that I should glory, save in the cross of our Lord Jesus Christ' (Gal. 6:14). The chorus is already loud, but it will be louder. For John tells us in his vision that: 'I beheld and I heard the voice of many angels round about the throne and the beasts and the elders: and the number of them was ten thousand times ten thousand, and thousands of thousands; saying with a loud voice, Worthy is the Lamb that was slain to receive power, and riches, and wisdom, and strength, and honour, and glory, and blessing. And every creature which is in heaven, and on the earth, and under the earth, and such as are in the sea, and all that are in them, heard I saying, Blessing, and honour, and glory, and power, be unto Him that sitteth upon the throne, and unto the Lamb for ever and ever' (Rev. 5:11-13). God grant that we may find ourselves among the blessed throng. We have but to believe on Him, to yield ourselves to Him, and to begin to make of Him our only boast here and now, and it is assured.

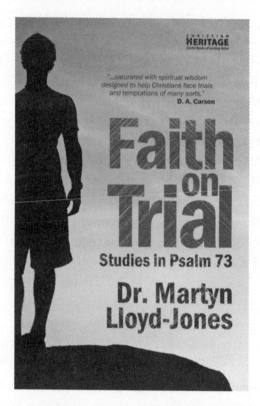

*"...saturated with spiritual wisdom
designed to help Christians face trials
and temptations of many sorts."*
D. A. Carson

Faith on Trial

Studies in Psalm 73

Dr. Martyn Lloyd-Jones

FAITH ON TRIAL

Studies in Psalm 73

Martyn Lloyd-Jones

Why do good people suffer unjustly - and yet others get away with it? The Psalmist, Asaph, dealt with this very problem in Psalm 73 – one that has often perplexed and discouraged God's people. Asaph reveals his own 'no-holds-barred' feelings and leads us step by step from near-despair to final assurance. For this reason it has always appealed to preachers and counsellors.

An excellent book for those struggling with, or wondering about, injustice in the world.

'When this book first appeared in 1965, I was an undergraduate reading chemistry and mathematics. I recall thinking as I read the book that this Lloyd-Jones chap (whom at that point I still had not met) had a God-given ability to meditate on a text, and ponder it within the framework of the entire Bible. I have not changed my mind, but I would now add as well that his exposition of Psalm 73 is saturated with spiritual wisdom designed to help Christians face trials and temptations of many sorts. I am very thankful to God to see this book come back into print.'

Don Carson,
Trinity Evangelical Divinity School, Deerfield, Illinois

'...if there is anything that struck me forcibly when I first read Faith on Trial..., it was as I verbalized to myself: 'This man really loves people. Why, he could love me.' ...It was this love that took him into the practice of medicine and from medicine to preaching... Those who sat in the pews at Aberavon, and later at Westminster and throughout the United Kingdom as he preached widely, knew that the "little man" preaching to them really cared about them.'

Thomas N. Smith,
Randolph Street Baptist Church, Charleston, West Virginia

ISBN 978-1-84550-375-8

LIFE OF FAITH

WHAT HAS GOD DONE FOR YOU?

A.W. PINK

The Life of Faith

What has God done for you?

A W Pink

What is the purpose of our lives?

God's design is that he might be glorified and that those he has chosen might be saved to have abundant life. The life of faith is lived in the light of this truth: so that Christians must remember lack of growth brings God no honour, prayerlessness gives no glory. Yet, positively God works in the believer through Scripture to prepare them for glory and to give them happiness here and now.

A. W. Pink looks at what God has done for us, why he has done this and how we should respond. He gives us marks of grace to look for in ourselves and reassurance as to the help God provides.

'... *biblical exposition with considerable emphasis on experimental godliness. Pink is often at his best when expounding Scripture characters.*'

Bill Black,
The Banner of Truth

A. W. Pink (1886-1952) was born in England and converted in his 20's. He was called to a pastorate in Colorado until 1921, after which he decided to concentrate on writing and speaking at conferences. The next year he started a monthly magazine 'Studies in the scriptures' which he edited until his death.

ISBN 978-1-85792-047-5

FELLOWSHIP FAITH

DEVIL REGENERATION

DEATH 18 WORDS

MEDIATOR ELECTION

GRACE RECONCILIATION

THE MOST IMPORTANT WORDS
YOU WILL EVER KNOW LORD

MORTIFICATION

SANCTIFICATION

HOLINESS JUSTIFICATION

WORLD J. I. PACKER

SIN SCRIPTURE

REVELATION

18 Words

The most important words you will ever know

J I Packer

If the modern world can be characterised by one thing it is probably the enormous increase in the number of words around - but that increase has also been accompanied by a seemingly corresponding decrease in understanding. It is the irony of the information age that instead of bringing clarity it has raised uninformed opinion to the same level as truth.

The church has also not been faultless. Rather than discuss ideas in order to come to some settled agreement, the church has been characterised as trying to make words mean different things in order to accommodate differences.

But the church should be a beacon of light to the world. The church has the words of eternal life.

J. I. Packer is a master wordsmith. He is also gifted with the ability of showing where truth lies in complicated reasoning. These skills combine to make Words from God a fascinating read — and a life-changing one.

The 18 words are Death, Devil, Election, Faith, Fellowship, Grace, Holiness, Justification, Lord, Mediator, Mortification, Reconciliation, Regeneration, Revelation, Sanctification, Scripture, Sin & World.

Jim Packer was named by Time Magazine as one of the 25 most influential evangelicals alive. He is the Board of Governor's Professor of Theology at Regent College, Vancouver, BC, Canada.

ISBN 978-1-84550-327-7

A
NEW
INNER
RELISH

CHRISTIAN MOTIVATION
in the THOUGHT *of*
JONATHAN EDWARDS

DANE ORTLUND

A New Inner Relish

Christian Motivation in the Thought of Jonathan Edwards

Dane Ortlund

'As I read the author's words on America's foremost theologian of his time, I found myself praying, "Oh God, send a new awakening, and begin it in me!"

Richard Bewes,
Former Rector of All Souls Church, Langham Place, London

'There are many books that promise to reveal Jonathan Edwards' insight into the Christian life. This book delivers. Dane Ortlund, artfully using the incisive and perennial thought of Edwards, points us to a Christian obedience that is indeed a whole hearted delight.'

Stephen J. Nichols,
Lancaster Bible College and Graduate School, Lamcaster, Pennslyvania

'Dane does a marvelous job of demonstrating how the "new sense of the heart," divinely and graciously imparted by God, governs Edwards' understanding of motivation in Christian obedience. I highly recommend Ortlund's clear and insightful study of it.'

Sam Storms,
Bridgeway Church, Oklahoma City, Oklahoma

'Dane Ortlund has sat at the feet of Jonathan Edwards and has learned much of what moved Edwards to be the person he was As we read these pages, we will be led to the same internal relish for God that transformed Edwards' life, theology, and ministry. Like Edwards we will be powerfully drawn by "the beauty of holiness".'

David B. Calhoun,
Covenant Theological Seminary, St. Louis, Missouri

Dane Ortlund is currently studying at Wheaton College for his PhD after studying and working at Covenant Theological Seminary. He is married to Stacey and they have a son.

ISBN 978-1-84550-349-9

CHRISTIAN FOCUS PUBLICATIONS
publishes books for all ages

Our mission statement –

STAYING FAITHFUL
In dependence upon God we seek to help make His infallible Word, the Bible, relevant. Our aim is to ensure that the Lord Jesus Christ is presented as the only hope to obtain forgiveness of sin, live a useful life and look forward to heaven with Him.

REACHING OUT
Christ's last command requires us to reach out to our world with His gospel. We seek to help fulfil that by publishing books that point people towards Jesus and help them develop a Christ-like maturity. We aim to equip all levels of readers for life, work, ministry and mission.

Books in our adult range are published in three imprints.

Christian Focus contains popular works including biographies, commentaries, basic doctrine and Christian living. Our children's books are also published in this imprint.

Mentor focuses on books written at a level suitable for Bible College and seminary students, pastors, and other serious readers. The imprint includes commentaries, doctrinal studies, examination of current issues and church history.

Christian Heritage contains classic writings from the past.

Christian Focus Publications Ltd,
Geanies House, Fearn, Ross-shire,
IV20 1TW, Scotland, United Kingdom
info@christianfocus.com

For details of our titles visit us on our website
www.christianfocus.com